FamilyCircle®

easy
Crochet
50 Fashion and Home Projects

FamilyCircle®

easy
Crochet
50 Fashion and Home Projects

Sixth&Spring Books
New York

Sixth&Spring Books
233 Spring Street
New York, NY 10013

Editorial Director
Trisha Malcolm

Book Editor
Michelle Lo

Art Director
Chi Ling Moy

Book Publishing Coordinator
Cara Beckerich

Copy Editors
Daryl Brower
Jean Guirguis

Yarn Editor
Veronica Manno

Technical Editors
Carla Scott
Karen Greenwald
Pat Harste

Production Manager
David Joinnides

President and Publisher, Sixth&Spring Books
Art Joinnides

Family Circle Magazine

Editor-in-Chief
Susan Kelliher Ungaro

Executive Editor
Barbara Winkler

Creative Director
Diane Lamphron

Library of Congress Catalog-in-Publication Data

Family circle easy crochet : 50 fashion and home projects.-- 1st ed.
      p.cm.
      ISBN 1-931543-35-6 (hardcover)
      ISBN-10: 1-931543-95-X, ISBN-13: 978-931543-95-8 (paper)

      1. Crocheting--Patterns. I. Title: Easy crochet. II. Family circle.

TT825 .F55 2003
746.43'4'041--dc21

                                                                    2002044561

Manufactured in China

Table of Contents

Fall Favorites

Get ready for sweater weather.

Worth Repeating

for intermediate crocheters

Gail Diven's matching mother-daughter sweaters make crocheting twice as nice. The simple silhouette is easy to stitch and embellished with cleverly created flowers—a button center surrounded by lazy daisy petals. "Worth Repeating" first appeared in the Fall '98 issue of *Family Circle Easy Knitting* magazine.

MATERIALS

■ *Wintuk* by Caron International, 3$\frac{1}{2}$oz/100g balls, each approx 213yd/196m (acrylic)

Woman's sweater

5 (6, 6, 6, 7, 7) of #3081 violet

■ 1 skein embroidery floss by Susan Bates in #0186 lt turquoise

■ 1 skein each DMC Embroidery floss in #068 bright pink and #0216 green

■ One each sizes G/6 (4.5mm) and I/9 (5.5mm) crochet hooks OR SIZE TO OBTAIN GAUGE

■ Seven $\frac{3}{4}$"/20mm buttons

■ Thirty four $\frac{1}{2}$"/13mm buttons

■ Yarn needle

Girl's sweater

3 (3, 4, 4, 5) balls in #3032 rosewine

■ 1 skein embroidery floss by Susan Bates in gold #0347

■ 1 skein each embroidery floss by Anchor in bright pink #068 and turquoise/green #0189

■ One each sizes G/6 (4.5mm) and I/9 (5.5mm) crochet hooks OR SIZE TO OBTAIN GAUGE

■ Six $\frac{3}{4}$"/20mm buttons

■ Eighteen $\frac{1}{2}$"/13mm buttons

■ Yarn needle

SIZES

Woman's sweater

Sized for X-Small (Small, Medium, Large, X-Large, XX-Large). Shown in size Medium.

Girl's sweater

Sized for Child's 2 (4, 6, 8, 10). Shown in size 4 .

FINISHED MEASUREMENTS

Woman's sweater

■ Bust 36$\frac{1}{2}$ (38, 39$\frac{1}{2}$, 41$\frac{1}{2}$, 44$\frac{1}{2}$, 48)"/92.5 (96.5, 100.5, 105.5, 113, 122)cm

■ Length 17 (19, 19, 20$\frac{1}{2}$, 22, 24)"/43.5 (48.5, 48.5, 52, 56, 61)cm

■ Upper arm 11 (12$\frac{1}{2}$, 12$\frac{1}{2}$, 13, 14, 15$\frac{1}{2}$)"/28 (32, 32, 33, 35.5, 39.5)cm

Girl's sweater

■ Chest 31 (32$\frac{1}{2}$, 34, 36, 38)"/78.5 (82.5, 86.5, 91.5, 96.5)cm

■ Length 13 (13, 14, 15, 17)"/33 (33, 35.5, 38, 43)cm

■ Upper arm 10 (10$\frac{1}{2}$, 11, 11$\frac{1}{2}$, 12$\frac{1}{2}$)"/25.5 (26.5, 28, 29, 32)cm

GAUGE

Both sweaters

13 sts and 17 rows to 4"/10cm in sc using size I/9 (5.5mm) crochet hook.

TAKE TIME TO CHECK YOUR GAUGE.

Note

All sc are referred to as sts.

WOMAN'S SWEATER

BACK

With size I/9 (5.5mm) crochet hook, ch 59 (61, 65, 67, 73, 79). **Row 1 (RS)** Sc in second ch from hook and in each ch st across—58 (60, 64, 66, 72, 78) sc. Ch 1, turn. Cont to work in sc until piece measures 9 (10, 10, 11, 12, 13)"/23 (25.5, 25.5, 28, 30.5, 33)cm from beg, end with a WS row. Do not ch, turn.

Armhole shaping

Next row (RS) Sl st in 4 (4, 4, 5, 5, 6) sts, pull up a lp in each of next 2 sc, yo and pull through all 3 lps on hook (dec 1 sc), sc across to last 6 (6, 6, 7, 7, 8) sts, dec 1 sc, leave rem sts unworked. Ch 1, turn **Next row** Dec 1 sc, sc across to last 2 sts, dec 1 sc—46 (48, 52, 52, 58, 62) sts. Cont to work in sc until armhole measures 7 (8, 8, 8$\frac{1}{2}$, 9, 10)"/18 (20.5, 20.5, 21.5, 23, 25.5)cm, end with a WS row. Do not ch, turn.

Shoulder and neck shaping

Next row (RS) Sl st in first 4 (4, 3, 3, 5, 4) sts, ch 1, sc to last 4 (4, 3, 3, 5, 4) sts, leave these sts unworked. Ch 1 turn. Cont to shape shoulder with 3 (3, 4, 4, 4, 5) sts left unworked at each end of next 3 rows and AT SAME TIME, leave center 16 (18, 18, 18, 20, 20) sts unworked for neck, then dec 1 sc each side of neck edge every row twice. Fasten off each side.

(Continued on page 10)

LEFT FRONT

With size I/9 (5.5mm) crochet hook, ch 30 (31, 32, 34, 36, 38). **Row 1 (RS)** Sc in second ch from hook and in each ch st across—29 (30, 31, 33, 35, 37) sc. Work in sc until piece measures same as back to armhole. Shape armhole as for back at beg of RS rows—23 (24, 25, 26, 28, 29) sts. Cont to work in sc until armhole measures 5 (6, 6, 6½, 7, 8)"/12.5 (15, 15, 16.5, 18, 20.5)cm, end with a WS row.

Neck shaping

Next row (RS) Sc across to last 4 sts, sl st in next st, leave rem 3 sts unworked. Ch 1, turn. **Next row** Skip sl st, sc in each st across. Cont to work, dec 1 st at neck edge every row until 13 (13, 15, 15, 17, 19) sts rem. Work shoulder shaping as for back.

RIGHT FRONT

Work as for left front, reversing shaping.

SLEEVES

With size I/9 (5.5mm) crochet hook, ch 31 (33, 33, 35, 35, 37). **Row 1 (RS)** Sc in second ch from hook and in each ch st across—30 (32, 32, 34, 34, 36) sc. Cont to work in sc, inc 1 st each side every 10 rows 3 (4, 4, 4, 6, 7) times—36 (40, 40, 42, 46, 50) sts. Cont until piece measures 17 (17, 17½, 18, 18, 18½)"/43 (43, 44.5, 45.5, 45.5, 47)cm from beg, end with a WS row. Do not ch, turn.

Cap shaping

Next row (RS) Sl st in first 4 (4, 4, 4, 5, 6) sts, dec 1 sc, sc across to last 6 (6, 6, 6, 7, 8) sts, dec 1 sc, leave rem 4 (4, 4, 4, 5, 6) sts unworked. **Next row** Sc in each sc. **Dec row** Dec 1 sc, sc in each sc to last 2 sts, dec 1 sc. Rep last 2 rows until 10 sts rem. Fasten off.

FINISHING

Block pieces lightly. Sew shoulder seams. Set in sleeves. Sew side and sleeve seams.

Front band

With RS facing, and size I/9 (95.5mm) crochet hook, join yarn at left front neck edge. Work sc evenly spaced along front edge to lower edge. Ch 1, turn. Sc in each sc for 3 more rows. Ch 1, do not turn. Place markers for 7 buttons evenly spaced along left front edge. Work sc along lower edge to lower right front corner, ch 1, work sc from right front lower edge to neck edge. Ch 1, turn. Work 1 row in sc along right front. Ch 1 turn. Sc to right front neck edge, working buttonholes opposite markers by ch 2, skip 2 sts. Ch 1, turn. Sc to right front lower edge, working 2 sc in each ch-2 sp. Ch 1, turn. Sc to right front neck edge. Ch 1, do not turn. Work sc evenly spaced along neck edge, sl st to first st. Change to smaller hook and ch 1. With RS facing, work 1 row of reverse sc in every sc around, sl st to first st. Fasten off. Sew buttons in place. Work lazy daisy flowers (see page 125) randomly placed using 40"/102cm strands of each embroidery floss, around sweater in assorted colors. Using embroidery floss, sew a small button in center of each flower.

GIRL'S SWEATER

Note

All sc are referred to as sts.

BODY

With size I/9 (5.5mm) crochet hook, ch 99 (103, 109, 115, 121). **Row 1 (RS)** Sc in second ch from hook and in each ch st across—98 (102, 108, 114, 120) sc. Continue to work in sc until piece measures 6 (6, 6½, 7, 8½)"/15 (15, 16.5, 19, 21.5)cm from beg, end with a WS row.

Divide for armhole shaping

Next row (RS) Sc in first 18 (19, 21, 22, 24) sts, pull up a lp in each of next 2 sc, yo and pull through all 3 lps on hook (dec 1 sc), for right front, sl st in next 8 (8, 8, 9, 9) sts, dec 1 sc, sc in next 38 (40, 42, 44, 46) sts for back, dec 1 sc, sl st in next 8 (8, 8, 9, 9) sts, dec 1 sc, sc rem 18 (19, 21, 22, 24) sts for left front. Ch 1, turn. Sc in first 17 (18, 20, 21, 23) sts, dec 1 sc, Ch 1, turn. Cont to work 18 (19, 21, 22, 24) sts until armhole measures 4 (4, 4½, 5, 5½)"/10 (10, 11.5, 12.5, 14)cm, end with a WS row.

Left front neck shaping

Next row (RS) Sc in each st to last 3 (3, 4, 5, 6) sts and leave sts unworked for neck edge. Ch 1, turn. Dec 1 sc, sc across row. Cont to dec 1 st at neck edge every row until 12 (13, 14, 15, 16) sts rem. Cont to work sc until armhole measures 6 (6, 6½, 7, 7½)"/15 (15, 16.5, 18, 19)cm, end with a WS row. Do not ch, turn.

Shoulder shaping

Next row (RS) Sl st in first 3 (4, 4, 3, 4) sts, ch 1, sc to end. Ch 1, turn. Cont to shape shoulder with 3 (3, 4, 4, 4) sts left unworked once and 3 (3, 3, 4, 4) sts twice.

Back

From WS join yarn and dec 1 sc, sc across 36 (38, 40, 42, 44) sts, dec 1 sc. Cont to work across sts of back until armhole measures same as front. Work shoulder shaping as for left front on 12 (13, 14, 15, 16) sts, and AT SAME TIME, leave center 10 sts unworked for neck, then dec 1 sc each side of neck every row twice. Fasten off each side.

Right front neck and shoulder shaping

From WS, join yarn, work as for left front, reversing neck and shoulder shaping.

SLEEVES

With size I/9 (5.5mm) crochet hook, ch 27 (27, 29, 29, 31). **Row 1 (RS)** Sc in second ch from hook and in each ch st across—26 (26, 28, 28, 30) sc. Work in sc, inc 1 st each side every 6 rows 3 (4, 4, 5, 5) times—32 (34, 36, 38, 40) sts. Cont until piece measures 12 (12, 12½, 13, 14)"/30.5 (30.5, 32, 33, 35.5)cm from beg, end with a WS row. Do not ch, turn.

Cap shaping

Next row (RS) Sl st in first 3 (4, 4, 4, 4) sts, dec 1 sc, sc across to last 5 (6, 6, 6, 6) sts, dec 1 sc, leave rem 3 (4, 4, 4, 4) sts unworked—24 (24, 26, 28, 30) sts. Work 1 row even. Dec 1 sc each side of next row. Rep last 2 rows until 10 sts rem. Fasten off.

FINISHING

Block pieces lightly. Sew shoulder seams. Set in sleeves. Sew side and sleeve seams.

Front band

With RS facing and size I/9 (5.5mm) crochet hook, join yarn at left front neck edge. Work sc evenly spaced along front edge to lower edge. Ch 1, turn. Sc in each sc for 3 more rows. Ch 1, do not turn. Place markers for 6 buttons evenly spaced along left front edge. Work sc along lower edge to lower right front corner, ch 1, work sc from right front lower edge to neck edge. Ch 1, turn. Work 1 row in sc along right front. Ch 1 turn. Sc to right front neck edge, working buttonholes opposite markers by ch 2, skip 2 sts. Ch 1, turn. Sc to right front lower edge, working 2 sc in each ch-2 sp. Ch 1, turn. Sc to right front neck edge. Ch 1, do not turn. Work sc evenly spaced along neck edge, sl st to first st. Change to smaller hook and ch 1. With RS facing, work 1 row of reverse sc in every sc around, sl st to beginning st. Fasten off. Sew buttons in place. Using strands of embroidery floss, each 40"/101.5cm long, work lazy daisy flowers randomly placed around sweater in assorted colors. Using embroidery floss, sew a small button in center of each flower.

WOMAN'S SWEATER

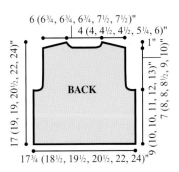

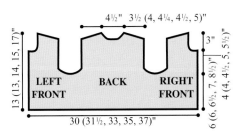

GIRL'S SWEATER

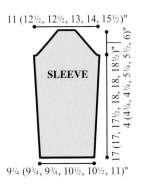

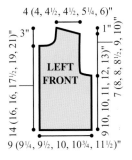

Laced with Grace

for advanced crocheters

Openwork floral bands lend old-fashioned romance to Mari Lynn Patrick's ultra-feminine lace cardigan. Hem, cuffs and collar are edged in soft scallops. "Laced with Grace" first appeared in the Fall '98 issue of *Family Circle Easy Knitting* magazine.

MATERIALS

- *Red Heart® Super Sport* by Coats & Clark™, 5oz/143g skeins, each approx 500yd/461m (acrylic)
  4 (4, 5, 5) skeins in #775 raspberry
  For sizes Medium and X-Large
- Size G/6 (4.5mm) crochet hook OR SIZE TO OBTAIN GAUGE
  For sizes Small and Large
- Size F/5 (4mm) crochet hook OR SIZE TO OBTAIN GAUGE.
- Nine ½"/13mm buttons

SIZES

Sized for Small (Medium, Large, X-Large). Shown in size Medium.

FINISHED MEASUREMENTS

- Bust (buttoned) 35 (38, 44, 47)"/89 (96.5, 111.5, 119)cm
- Length 20 (20½, 21, 21½)"/51 (52, 53.5, 54.5)cm
- Upper arm 13½ (14, 15½, 16½)"/34 (35.5, 39.5, 42)cm

GAUGE

Note

Be sure to get given gauge for your chosen size.
For Small and Large sizes

- 18 dc to 4"/10cm and 7 pat rows to 3"/7.5cm using size F/5 (4mm) hook
  For Medium and X-Large sizes
- 17 dc to 4"/10cm and 7 pat rows to 3"/7.5cm using size G/6 (4.5mm) hook.
TAKE TIME TO CHECK YOUR GAUGE.

STITCHES USED

Lace Pattern Stitch

(Ch a multiple of 10 ch plus 2)
For gauge swatch, ch 32
Row 1 Work 1 dc in 4th ch from hook and in each ch to end - 30 dc (for swatch). Turn.
Row 2 Ch 3 (counts as 1 dc), skip first dc, dc in each dc to end. Turn.
Row 3 Ch 6, *skip next 4 dc, in next dc work 1 sc, [ch 5, 1 sc] 3 times for a flower, ch 3, skip 4 dc, 1 dc in next dc, ch 3; rep from *, end skip 4 dc, 1 flower in next dc, ch 3, skip 4 dc, 1 dc in top of t-ch. Turn.
Row 4 Ch 5, 1 sc, ch 5 and 1 sc in first dc, *ch 3, 1 dc in center ch-5 sp of next flower, ch 3, 1 flower in next dc; rep from *, end ch 3, 1 dc in center ch-5 sp of next flower, ch 3, 1 sc, ch 5, 1 sc, ch 2 and 1 dc in 3rd st of t-ch. Turn.
Row 5 Ch 1, 1 sc in first ch-2 sp, *ch 4, 1 sc in dc, ch 4, 1 sc in center ch-5 sp of next flower; rep from *, end last rep with 1 sc in last ch-5 sp. Turn.
Row 6 Ch 3, 3 dc in first ch-4 sp, * 1 dc in next sc, 4 dc in next ch-4 sp; rep from *, end 1 dc in last sc—30 dc. Turn.
Rep rows 2-6 for lace pat st.

BACK

With size F/5 (G/6, F/5, G/6)/4 (4.5, 4, 4.5)mm hook, ch 82 (82, 102, 102). Work in pat st on 8 (8, 10, 10) pat reps or 80 (80, 100, 100) dc until piece measures 13"/33cm or 30 rows from beg, end with pat row 5.

Armhole shaping

*Pat row 6 (RS) Ch 1 (instead of ch 3), 4 sl sts into each ch of ch-4 sp, sl st in next sc, ch 3, 3 dc in ch-4 sp, 1 dc in next sc, *4 dc in next ch-4 sp, 1 dc in next sc; rep from * to last sc and ch-4 sp, dec 1 dc in last sc and ch-4 sp (dec 1 dc by yo and pull up a lp in sc, yo and pull through 2 lps, yo and pull up a lp in sp, yo and pull through 2 lps, yo and pull through all 3 lps), leave rem sts unworked—5 sts dec each end of row—70 (70, 90, 90) dc. Turn. **Row 2** Ch 3, skip first dc, dec 1 dc in next 2 dc, dc to last 2 dc, dec 1 dc in last 2 dc—68 (68, 88, 88) dc. **Row 3** Ch 6, skip 3 dc, dc in next dc, ch 3, rep from * of pat row 3, end with 1 dc in top of t-ch. **Row 4** Ch 3, skip first ch 3-sp, 1 sc, ch 2, 1 sc in 2nd dc, rep from * of pat row 4, end last rep by sc, ch 2, sc in last dc. **Row 5** Work pat row 5, end last rep with sc in last ch-2 sp. ***Row 6** Work pat row 6—60 (60, 80, 80) dc. Work even until armhole measures 7 (7½, 7½, 7½)"/18 (19, 19, 19)cm, ending with pat row 6 (2, 2, 2). Work 0 (0, 1, 2) more rows even in dc. Armhole measures 7 (7½, 8, 8½)"/18 (19, 20.5, 21.5)cm. Fasten off.

LEFT FRONT

With chosen hook size, ch 42 (42, 52, 52). Work in pat st on 4 (4, 5, 5) pat reps or 40 (40, 50, 50) dc until same length as back to armhole.

Armhole shaping

Shape armhole as on right edge of back—30 (30, 40, 40) dc. Work even until armhole measures 4½"/11.5cm, end with pat row 5.

Neck shaping

Pat row 6 (RS) Work dc as on pat row 6 to last 2 ch—4 sps, ch 2, sl st in 2nd ch of next ch-4 sp, leave rem sps unworked. Turn. **Row 2** Ch 3, skip ch-2 sp, 1 sc in next dc, 1 hdc in next dc, ch 3, skip 3 dc, 1 dc in each of next 15 (15, 25, 25) dc.

(Continued on page 129)

Mommy and Me

for intermediate crocheters

Mari Lynn Patrick's sweetly styled pullovers are sure to win smiles from any mother/daughter team. Both feature an Empire bodice ending in a body-skimming pattern of lace stitches. Mom's version sports a flattering V-neck; daughter's is finished with a three-button front opening. "Mommy and Me" first appeared in the Fall '98 issue of *Family Circle Easy Knitting* magazine.

MATERIALS

▪ *Red Heart® Sport* by Coats & Clark™, 2½oz/70g skeins, each approx 250yd/230m (acrylic)

Woman's sweater

8 (9, 10, 10) skeins in #508 med green

Girl's sweater

5 (5, 6, 7) skeins in #683 lt green

▪ Three ½"/13mm buttons

Both sweaters

▪ One each sizes G/6, H/8 and I/9 (4.5, 5 and 5.5mm) crochet hooks OR SIZES TO OBTAIN GAUGES.

SIZES

Woman's sweater

Sized for Small (Medium, Large, X-Large). Shown in size Large.

Girl's sweater

Sized for Child's 4 (6, 8, 10). Shown in size 6.

FINISHED MEASUREMENTS

Woman's sweater

▪ Bust 36½ (41, 46, 50)"/92.5 (104, 117, 127)cm

▪ Length 28½ (29, 29½, 30)"/72.5 (73.5, 75, 76)cm

▪ Upper arm 13¾ (15, 16, 17)"/35 (38, 40.5, 43)cm

Girl's sweater

▪ Chest 29 (32, 35, 40)"/73.5 (81, 89, 101.5)cm

▪ Length 17½ (18½, 20½, 22)"/44.5 (47.5, 52, 55.5)cm

▪ Upper arm 11¾ (12¼, 13½, 14½)"/30 (31, 34, 37)cm

GAUGES

Woman's sweater

▪ 4 lace pats to 4½"/11.5cm using size G/6 (4.5mm) hook

▪ 4 lace pats to 5"/12.5cm using size H/8 (5mm) hook

▪ 4 lace pats to 5½"/14cm using size I/9 (5.5mm) hook

(For lace pat there is no stated row gauge. Work pat to length measurements.)

▪ 14 sc and 16 rows to 4"/10cm over sc pat st using size I/9 (5.5mm) hook.

Girl's sweater

▪ 4 lace pats to 5½"/14cm using size I/9 (5.5mm) hook.

▪ 15 sc and 17 rows to 4"/10cm over sc pat st using size H/8 (5mm) hook.

TAKE TIME TO CHECK YOUR GAUGES.

Note

For lace pat there is no stated row gauge. Work pat to length measurements.

STITCHES USED

Lace Pattern Stitch

(chain a multiple of 6 ch plus 1)

Note

To work gauge swatch, ch 25.

Row 1 Skip 3 chs, 3 dc in next ch, *skip 2 chs, sc in next ch, skip 2 chs, 3 dc in next ch; rep from *, end skip 2 chs, sc in last ch—4 lace pats. Ch 3, turn.

Row 2 3 dc in first sc of previous row, *sc in top of last dc of 3-dc group, ch 2, 3-dc in next sc; rep from *, end sc in last dc. Ch 3, turn.

Rep row 2 for lace pat st.

Sc Pattern Stitch

(chain an even number of ch)

Row 1 2 sc in 2nd ch from hook, *skip 1 ch, 2 sc in next ch; rep from * to end. Ch 1, turn.

Row 2 *Skip 1 sc, 2 sc in next sc; rep from * to end. Ch 1, turn.

Rep row 2 for sc pat st.

WOMAN'S SWEATER

BACK

With size I/9 (5.5mm) hook, ch 97 (109, 121, 133). Work in lace pat st on 16 (18, 20, 22) lace pats for 6"/15.5cm. Change to size H/8 (5mm) hook and cont in lace pat st for 6"/15.5cm more. Change to size G/6 (4.5mm) hook and cont in lace pat for 5"/12.5cm more. **Next row (RS)** Ch 1, *1 sc in next sc, 1 sc in next dc, skip 1 dc, 1 sc in next dc, 1 sc in ch-2 sp; rep from *, end 1 sc in next sc, 1 sc in each of last 3 dc—64 (72, 80, 88) sc. Fasten off. **Next row (RS)** Rejoin yarn at beg of row, ch 5 (counts as 1 tr), skip first sc, 1 tr in back lps only of each sc across. Fasten off. **Next row (RS)** Rejoin yarn at beg of row, ch 1, work 1 sc in back lps only of each tr across. Ch 1, turn. Change to size I/9 (5.5mm) hook, and beg with row 2, work in sc pat st for 9 rows or 2¼"/6cm. Piece measures approx 20¼"/51.5cm from beg. Do not ch, turn.

Armhole shaping

Next row (RS) Sl st across first 4 sts, ch 1 and work pat to last 4 sts, leave these sts unworked. Work 1 row even. **Next row (RS)** Work sc pat to

(Continued on page 16)

last 2 sts, leave these sts unworked. Rep last row (dec 2 sts at end of every row) 3 (5, 5, 7) times more—48 (52, 60, 64) sc. Work even until armhole measures 7½ (8, 8½, 9)"/19 (20.5, 21.5, 23)cm. Do not ch, turn.

Shoulder shaping

Next row (RS) Sl st across first 4 (5, 6, 7) sts, ch 1 and pat to last 4 (5, 6, 7) sts, leave these sts unworked. Ch 1, turn. Rep last row once more. Do not ch, turn. **Next row** Sl st across 5 (5, 7, 7) sts, ch 1 and work pat to last 5 (5, 7, 7) sts, leave these sts unworked. Fasten off 22 sts for back neck.

FRONT

Work as for back to armhole shaping.

Armhole and neck shaping

Next row (RS) Sl st across first 4 sts, ch 1 and work in pat until there are 27 (31, 35, 39) sts, leave center 2 sts unworked, join a 2nd skein of yarn and work to last 4 sts, leave these 4 sts unworked. Cont to shape armhole as on back and working both sides at once, dec 2 sts each side of neck every 4th row twice, every 6th row 3 times—13 (15, 19, 21) sts rem each side. When same length as back, shape shoulders as for back.

SLEEVES

With size I/9 (5.5mm) hook, ch 49. Work in lace pat st on 8 lace pats for 4 rows. Change to size H/8 (5mm) hook and work in lace pat st for 4 more rows. Change to size G/6 (4.5mm) hook and cont in lace pat until piece measures 5"/12.5cm from beg. **Next row (RS)** Ch 1, *1 sc in next sc, 1 sc in next dc, skip 1 dc, 1 sc in next

dc, 1 sc in ch-2sp; rep from *, end 1 sc in next sc, 1 sc in each of last 3 dc—32 sc. Fasten off. Join yarn at beg of row and work 1 row tr in back lps only and 1 row sc in back lps only on these 32 sc as on back. Change to size I/9 (5.5mm) hook and cont in sc pat st inc 2 pat sts each side every 8th (6th, 6th, 6th) row 4 (5, 6, 7) times—48 (52, 56, 60) sc. Work even until piece measures 18"/45.5cm from beg. Do not ch, turn.

Cap shaping

Next row (RS) Sl st across first 4 sts, ch 1 and work pat to last 4 sts, leave these sts unworked. Work 1 (1, 0, 0) row even. **Next row** Work pat to last 2 sts leave these sts unworked. Rep last row (dec 2 sts at end of every row) 3 times more. Then, dec 4 sts at end of next 8 rows. Fasten off rem 0 (4, 8, 12) sts.

FINISHING

Block very lightly. Sew shoulder seams. Sew sleeves into armholes. Sew side and sleeve seams. With size G/6 (4.5mm) hook, work 1 rnd sc evenly around neck. **Next rnd** Ch 5, work 1 tr in back lp of each sc, dec 2 tr at center v-neck. **Next rnd** Work 1 sc in back lp of each tr. Fasten off.

GIRL'S SWEATER
BACK

With size I/9 (5.5mm) hook, ch 67 (73, 79, 91). Work in lace pat st on 11 (12, 13, 15) lace pats for 9 (9½, 11, 12)"/23 (24, 28, 30.5)cm. Change to size H/8 (5mm) hook. **Next row (RS)** Ch 1, *1 sc in next sc, 1 sc in each of next 3 dc, 1 sc in ch-

2 sp; rep from *, end 1 sc in next sc, 1 sc in each of last 3 dc—54 (59, 64, 74) sc. Fasten off. **Next row (RS)** Rejoin yarn at beg of row, ch 5 (counts as 1 tr), skip first sc, for all sizes except size 6, work 1 tr in back lps only of each sc across—54 (60, 64, 74) tr. Fasten off. **Next row (RS)** Rejoin yarn at beg of row, ch 1, inc 1 st at beg and end of row for size 8 only, work 1 sc in back lps only of each tr across—54 (60, 66, 74) sc. Ch 1, turn. Beg with row 2, work in sc pat st until piece measures 12 (12½, 14, 15)"/30.5 (32, 35.5, 38)cm from beg. Do not ch, turn.

Armhole shaping

Next row (RS) Sl st across first 2 sts, ch 1 and work pat to last 2 sts, leave these sts unworked. Work 1 row even. **Next row (RS)** Work sc pat to last 2 sts, leave these sts unworked. Ch 1, turn. Rep last row (dec 2 sts at end of every row) 5 (5, 7, 9) times more—38 (44, 46, 50) sc. Work even until armhole measures 5½ (6, 6½, 7)"/14 (15.5, 16.5, 17.5)cm. Fasten off.

FRONT

Work as for back until armhole measures ½ (½, 1, 1½)"/1.25 (1.25, 2.5, 4)cm.

Placket opening

Work to center 4 sts, leave these sts unworked. Join a 2nd skein of yarn and work to end. Working both sides at once, cont armhole shaping, then work even until armhole measures 3¾ (4¼, 4½, 5)"/9.5 (11, 11.5, 12.5)cm.

Neck shaping

Next row Work to last 4 sts of first side, leave these sts unworked; sl st across first 4 sts of 2nd side, ch 1 and work to end. Cont to dec 2 sts from each neck edge 1 (1, 2, 2) times more. When same length as back, fasten off 11 (14, 13, 15) sts each side for shoulders.

SLEEVES

With size I/9 (5.5mm) hook, ch 31. Work in lace pat on 6 lace pats for 2"/5cm. Work sc row and tr row as for back on 24 tr. On next sc row, work as for back, inc 0 (1, 1, 1) sc each side—24 (26, 26, 26) sc. Change to size H/8 (5mm) hook and cont in sc pat st inc 2 sts each side every 4th (6th, 6th, 6th) row 5 (5, 6, 7) times—44 (46, 50, 54) sts. Work even until piece measures 10½ (11½, 12½, 15)"/26.5 (29, 32, 38)cm from beg. Do not ch, turn.

Cap shaping

Next row (RS) Sl st across first 2 sts, ch 1 and work pat to last 2 sts, leave these 2 sts unworked. Work 1 row even. **Next row** Work pat to last 2 sts, leave these sts unworked. Ch 1, turn. Rep this row (dec 2 sts at end of every row) 9 times more. Leave 4 sts unworked at end of next 4 rows. Fasten off rem 4 (6, 10, 14) sts.

FINISHING

Block very lightly. Sew shoulder seams. Sew sleeves into armholes. Sew side and sleeve seams. With size G/6 (4.5mm) hook, work sc evenly around neck and placket edges working 3 sc in each corner. Cut yarn. Work 1 dc in back lps only of each sc, working 3 dc in corners. Fasten off. Work 3 ch-5 lps and sew under right placket. Sew on buttons.

WOMAN'S SWEATER

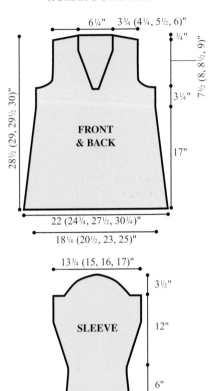

GIRL'S SWEATER

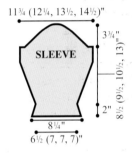

Aran Artistry
for intermediate crocheters

Gail Diven gives a tried-and-true classic a new twist by reworking a traditional Aran design in contemporary crochet cables, geometric patterning and whimsical bobbles. Minimal shaping makes it simple to stitch. "Aran Artistry" first appeared in the Winter '98/'99 issue of *Family Circle Easy Knitting* magazine.

MATERIALS
- *Debbie Bliss Merino DK* by Shepherd/Unique Kolours, $1^3/_4$oz/50g balls, each approx 119yd/100m (wool)
  14 (16, 18) balls in #200 blue
- Size G/6 (4.5mm) crochet hook OR SIZE TO OBTAIN GAUGE

SIZES
Sized for Small (Medium, Large). Shown in size Small.

FINISHED MEASUREMENTS
- Bust $36^1/_2$ ($39^1/_2$, $42^1/_2$)"/92.5 (100, 108)cm
- Length 21 ($21^1/_2$, 22)"/53.5 (54.5, 56)cm
- Upper arm $13^1/_4$ ($14^3/_4$, $15^3/_4$)"/33.5 (37.5, 40)cm

GAUGE
16 sts and 18 rows to 4"/10cm over sc using size G/6 (4.5mm) crochet hook.
TAKE TIME TO CHECK YOUR GAUGE.

STITCHES USED
Note
See Crochet Basics on page 124 for up-close details.

MB (Make Bobble)
*Yo, insert hook into next st, yo and draw lp through, yo and through 2 lps on hook; rep from * twice more, inserting hook into same st, yo and draw through 3 lps, yo and draw through last 2 lps.

FPDC (Front Post Double Crochet)
Yo and insert the hook from front to back to front around the post of the next stitch, but one row below, yo and draw lp through, complete dc.

3-st LT (Left Twist)
Skip the first post st, work the next 2 post sts, then go back to the first post st and complete the fpdc.

Notes
1 See page 129 for charted pat.

2 When working V-cable and diamond cable, work right twist fpdc to the right of the center fpdc and left twist fpdc to the left of the center fpdc (see Crochet Basics on page 124 for explanation of left and right twist).

BACK
Ch 74 (80, 86). Sc in 2nd ch from hook and in each ch to end—73 (79, 85) sc. Ch 1, turn.

Beg chart pats
Row 1 (WS) Work 8 (10, 12) sc, 5 sts V-cable, 3 (4, 4) sc, *3-st cable, 7 sts bobble pat, 3-st cable*, 15 (15, 17) sts diamond cable, rep between *'s once, 3 (4, 4) sc, 5 sts V-cable, 8 (10, 12) sc. Cont in pats as established until piece measures 11"/28cm from beg, end with a RS row.

Armhole shaping
Dec 1 sc each side on next row, then every row 3 (7, 9) times more, then every other row 18 (17, 17) times. Fasten off rem 29 (29, 31) sts for back neck.

FRONT
Work as for back until there are 37 (37, 39) sts.

Neck shaping
Cont armhole shaping, leave center 21 (21, 23) sts unworked for neck and working both sides at once with separate balls of yarn, dec 1 st at each neck edge every row 4 times.

SLEEVES
Ch 36 (38, 40). Sc in 2nd ch from hook and in each ch to end—35 (37, 39) sc. Ch 1, turn.

Beg chart pats
Row 1 (WS) Work 0 (1, 1) sc, 7 sts bobble pat, 3-st cable, 15 (15, 17) sts diamond cable, 3-st cable, 7 sts bobble pat, 0 (1, 1) sc. Cont in pats as established, inc 1 st each side (working incs into 3-st cable, then rem sts in sc) every 8th (6th, 6th) row 9 (11, 12) times—53 (59, 63) sts. Work even until piece measures 18 ($18^1/_2$, $18^1/_2$)"/45.5 (47, 47)cm from beg.

Cap shaping
Work same as back raglan armhole shaping. Fasten off rem 9 sts.

FINISHING
Block pieces to measurements. Sew shoulder seams. Set in sleeves. Sew side and sleeve seams.

(Continued on page 129)

Under Wraps

for intermediate crocheters

Chase away the autumn chill with Melissa Leapman's vintage-look shawl. Worked in an elegant shell stitch, it's the perfect layering piece for days when it's too cool to head out uncovered but not cold enough for a coat. "Under Wraps" first appeared in the Fall '00 issue of *Family Circle Easy Knitting* magazine.

MATERIALS

▦ *Angora Tweed* by Garnstudio/Aurora Yarns, 1³/₄oz/50g balls, each approx 162yd/150m (wool/angora)
7 balls in #10 white
▦ Sizes G/6 (4.5mm) crochet hook OR SIZE TO OBTAIN GAUGE

FINISHED MEASUREMENTS

▦ Approx 63" x 35"/160cm x 89cm

GAUGE

Each shell pat measures 1¹/₄"/3cm wide.
TAKE TIME TO CHECK YOUR GAUGE.

SHELL PATTERN

(Dc, ch 1, dc, ch 1, dc, ch 1, dc, ch 1, dc) into next st.

SHAWL

Ch 442.

Row 1 (RS) Sc into 2nd ch from hook, *skip next 4 ch, shell pat into next ch, skip next 4 ch, sc into next ch; rep from * to end. Ch 3, turn.

Row 2 Skip sc and first dc, sc into next ch-1 sp, ch 2, skip next dc, sc into next dc, *ch 2, skip next dc, dc into next ch-1 sp, ch 2, skip next (dc, sc, and dc), dc into next ch-1 sp, ch 2, skip next dc, sc into next dc; rep from * leaving last 2 dc and sc unworked. Ch 1, turn.

Row 3 Skip first sc and next dc, *shell into next ch-2 sp, sc into next sc, skip next ch-2 sp and next dc; rep from *, leaving last ch-2 sp and ch-3 t-ch unworked. Ch 3, turn.
Rep rows 2 and 3 until only one shell rem, ending with a row 3.

Next row Skip next dc, sc into next ch-1 sp, ch 3, skip next dc, sc into next dc, ch 3, skip next dc, sc into next ch-1 sp, *ch 3, skip next dc, sc into next dc, ch 3, skip next dc, sc into next ch-1 sp; rep from * along side, ending with ch 3, sk next dc, sc into last sc. Ch 6, turn.

Next row *Sc into next ch-sp, ch 4; rep from * around all three sides, ending with sc into next ch-sp, ch 3, dc into last st.
Fasten off.

Double Delights

for experienced crocheters

Stitch up a little sophistication times two. Tricia McKenzie's diamond-patterned tunics have drop shoulders and pretty shell-patterned edging. Length variations and a delicate drawstring option let you customize the look. "Double Delights" first appeared in the Fall '01 issue of *Family Circle Easy Knitting* magazine.

MATERIALS

▪ *Speed-Cro Sheen* by J & P Coats®/Coats & Clark™, 1.6oz/1.47g skeins each approx 100yd/91m (cotton)

  14 (15, 16) balls in #486 navy OR #61 natural

▪ F/5 (4mm) crochet hook OR SIZE TO OBTAIN GAUGE

SIZES

Sized for X-Small/Small (Medium/Large, X-Large) Shown in size X-Small/Small.

FINISHED MEASUREMENTS

▪ Bust 34 (42½, 51)"/86.5 (106.5, 129.5)cm

▪ Length 26½"/67 cm

▪ Upper arm 18"/46 cm

GAUGE

1 diamond pat rep to 4¼"/11cm wide and 8 rows of pat to 2¾"/7cm long using size F/5 (4mm) hook.

TAKE TIME TO CHECK YOUR GAUGE.

DIAMOND PATTERN FOR BACK AND FRONT

Ch a multiple of 16 plus 6.

Row 1 (RS) 1 sc in 2nd ch from hook, *skip 1 ch, 5 dc in next ch, skip 1 ch, 1 sc in next ch, ch 5, skip 3 ch, 1 sc in next ch; rep from *, end skip 1 ch, 5 dc in next ch, skip 1 ch, 1 sc in last ch. Ch 5, turn.

Row 2 *1 sc in 3rd of next 5 dc, ch 5, 1sc in next ch-5 sp, 5 dc in next sc, 1 sc in 3rd of next 5 dc, 5 dc in next sc, 1 sc in next ch-5 sp, ch 5; rep from *, end 1 sc in 3rd of next 5 dc, ch 2, 1 dc in last sc. Ch 1, turn.

Row 3 1 sc in first dc, *ch 5, 1 sc in next ch-5 sp, 5 dc in next sc, 1 sc in 3rd of next 5 dc, ch 5, 1 sc in 3rd of next 5 dc, 5 dc in next sc, 1 sc in next ch-5 sp; rep from *, end ch 5, 1 sc in t-ch. Ch 3, turn.

Row 4 2 dc in first sc, *1 sc in next ch-5 sp, 5 dc in next sc, 1 sc in 3rd of next 5 dc, ch 5, 1 sc in next ch-5 sp, ch 5, 1 sc in 3rd of next 5 dc, 5 dc in next sc; rep from *, end 1 sc in next ch-5 sp, 3 dc in last sc. Ch 1, turn.

Row 5 1 sc in first dc, *5 dc in next sc, 1 sc in 3rd of next 5 dc, ch 5, 1 sc in next ch-5 sp, 5 dc in next sc, 1 sc in next ch-5 sp, ch 5, 1 sc in 3rd of next 5 dc; rep from *, end 5 dc in next sc, 1 sc in top of t-ch. Ch 3, turn.

Row 6 2 dc in first sc, *1 sc in 3rd of next 5 dc, 5 dc in next sc, 1 sc in next ch-5 sp, ch 5, 1 sc in 3rd of next 5 dc, ch 5, 1 sc in next ch-5 sp, 5 dc in next sc; rep from *, end 1 sc in 3rd on next 5 dc, 3 dc in last sc. Ch 1, turn

Row 7 1 sc in first dc, *ch 5, 1 sc in 3rd of next 5 dc, 5 dc in next sc, 1 sc in next ch-5 sp, ch 5, 1 sc in next ch-5 sp, 5 dc in next sc, 1 sc in 3rd of next 5 dc; rep from *, end ch 5, 1 sc in top of t-ch. Ch 5, turn.

Row 8 *1 sc in next ch-5 sp, ch 5, 1 sc in 3rd of next 5 dc, 5 dc in next sc, 1 sc in next ch-5 sp, 5 dc in next sc, 1 sc in 3rd of next 5 dc, ch 5; rep from *, end 1 sc in next ch-5 sp, ch 2, 1 dc in the last sc. Ch 1, turn.

Row 9 1 sc in first dc, 5 dc in next sc, 1 sc in next ch-5 sp, ch 5, 1 sc in 3rd of next 5 dc, *5 dc in next sc, 1 sc in next ch-5 sp, ch 5, 1 sc in next ch-5 sp, 5 dc in next sc, 1 sc in next ch-5 sp**, ch 5, 1 sc in 3rd of next 5 dc; rep from *, end last

rep at ** in t-ch. Ch 5, turn.

Rep rows 2-9 for diamond pat for back and front.

DIAMOND PATTERN FOR SLEEVES (INCLUDING INCS)

Chain a multiple of 16 plus 6

Rows 1-3 Work as for diamond pat for back and front.

Row 4 4 dc in first sc, *1 sc in next ch-5 sp, 5 dc in next sc, 1 sc in 3rd of next 5 dc, ch 5, 1 sc in next ch-5 sp, ch 5, 1 sc in 3rd of next 5 dc, 5 dc in next sc; rep from *, end 1 sc in next ch-5 sp, 5 dc in last sc (1 half dc group inc'd at each side). Ch 5, turn.

Row 5 1 sc in 3rd of next 5 dc, *5 dc in next sc, 1 sc in 3rd of next 5 dc, ch 5, 1 sc in next ch-5 sp, 5 dc in next sc, 1 sc in next ch-5 sp, ch 5, 1 sc in 3rd of next 5 dc; rep from *, end 5 dc in next sc, 1 sc in 3rd of last 4 dc, ch 2, 1 dc in top of t-ch. Ch 1 turn.

Row 6 1 sc in first sc, *5 dc in next sc, 1 sc in 3rd of next 5 dc, 5 dc in next sc, 1 sc in next ch-5 sp, ch 5, 1 sc in 3rd of next 5 dc, ch 5, 1 sc in next ch-5 sp; rep from, end 5 dc in next sc, 1 sc in 3rd of next 5 dc, 5 dc in next sc, 1 sc in 3rd ch of t-ch. Ch 3 turn.

Row 7 2 dc in first sc, *1 sc in 3rd of next 5 dc, ch 5, 1sc in 3rd of next 5 dc, 5 dc in next sc, 1 sc in next ch-5 sp, ch 5, 1 sc in next ch-5 sp, 5 dc in

(Continued on page 24)

next sc; rep from *, end 1 sc in 3rd of next 5 dc, ch 5, 1 sc in 3rd of next 5 dc, 3 dc in next sc. Ch 3, turn.

Row 8 (2 dc, 1 sc) in first dc, *ch 5, 1 sc in next ch-5 sp, ch 5, 1 sc in 3rd of next 5 dc, 5 dc in next sc, 1 sc in next ch-5 sp, 5 dc in next sc, 1 sc in 3rd of next 5 dc; rep from *, end ch 5, 1 sc in next ch-5 sp, ch 5, (1 sc, 3 dc) in 3rd ch of t-ch (1 half dc group inc'd at each side). Ch 1 turn.

Row 9 1 sc in first dc, *ch 5, 1 sc in next ch-5 sp, 5 dc in next sc, 1 sc in next ch-5 sp, ch 5 **, 1 sc in 3rd of next 5 dc, 5 dc in next sc, 1 sc in 3rd of next 5 dc; rep from * ending last rep at **, 1 sc in top of t-ch. Ch 3, turn.

Row 10 2 dc in first sc, 1 sc in next ch-5 sp, *ch 5, 1 sc in 3rd of next 5 dc, ch 5, 1 sc in next ch-5 sp**, 5 dc in next sc, 1 sc in 3rd of next 5 ch, 5 dc in next sc, 1 sc in next ch-5 sp; rep from*, ending last rep at **, 3 dc in last sc. Ch 1 turn.

Row 11 1sc in first dc, *5 dc in next sc, 1 sc in next ch-5 sp, ch 5, 1 sc in next ch-5 sp, 5 dc in next sc, **1 sc in 3rd of next 5 dc, ch 5, 1sc in 3rd of next 5 dc; rep from * ending last rep at **, 1 sc in top of t-ch. Ch 5 turn.

Row 12 1 sc in 3rd of next 5 dc, *5 dc in next sc, 1 sc in next ch-5 sp, 5 dc in next sc, 1 sc in 3rd of next 5 dc**, ch 5, 1 sc in next ch-5 sp, ch 5, 1 sc in 3rd of next 5 dc; rep from * ending last rep at **, ch 2, 1 dc in last sc. Ch 1 turn.

Row 13 1 sc in first dc, *ch 5, 1 sc in 3rd of next 5 dc, 5 dc in next sc, 1 sc in 3rd of next 5 dc, ch 5, 1 sc in next ch-5 sp**, 5 dc in next sc, 1 sc in next ch-5 sp; rep from * ending last rep at **. Ch 5, turn.

Row 14 *1 sc in next ch-5 sp, 5 dc in next sc, 1 sc in 3rd of next 5 dc, 5 dc in next ch-5 sp**, ch 5, 1 sc in 3rd of next 5 dc, ch 5; rep from* ending last rep at **, ch 2, 1 dc in last sc. Ch 1, turn.

Row 15 1 sc in first dc, *5 dc in next sc, 1 sc in 3rd of next 5 dc, ch 5, 1 sc in 3rd of next 5 dc, 5 dc in next sc, 1 sc in next ch-5 sp **, ch 5, 1 sc in

next ch-5 sp; rep from * ending last rep at **. Ch 3, turn.

Row 16 4 dc in first sc, *1 sc in 3rd of next 5 dc, ch 5, 1 sc in next ch-5 sp, ch 5, 1 sc in 3rd of next 5 dc, 5 dc in next sc **, 1 sc in next ch-5 sp, 5 dc in next sc; rep from * ending last rep at ** (1 half dc group inc'd at each side). Ch 3, turn.

Row 17 2 dc in first sc, *1 sc in 3rd of next 5 dc, ch 5, 1 sc in next ch-5 sp, 5 dc in next sc, 1 sc in next ch-5 sp, ch 5, 1 sc in 3rd of next 5 dc**, 5 dc in next sc; rep from *, ending last rep at **, 3 dc in top of t-ch. Ch 1, turn.

Row 18 1 sc in first dc, *5 dc in next sc, 1 sc in next ch-5 sp, ch 5, 1 sc in 3rd of next 5 dc, ch 5, 1 sc in next ch-5 sp, 5 dc in next sc**, 1 sc in 3rd of next 5 dc; rep from * ending last rep at **, 1 sc in top of t-ch. Ch 5, turn.

Row 19 *1 sc in 3rd of next 5 dc, 5 dc in next sc, 1 sc in next ch-5 sp, ch 5, 1 sc in next ch-5 sp, 5 dc in next sc, 1 sc in 3rd of next 5 dc **, ch 5; rep from* ending last rep at **, ch 2, 1 dc in last sc. Ch 5, turn.

Row 20 1 sc in first dc, *ch 5, 1 sc in 3rd of next 5 dc, 5 dc in next sc, 1 sc in next ch-5 sp, 5 dc in next sc, 1 sc in 3rd of next 5 dc, ch 5, 1 sc in next ch-5 sp; rep from * end 2 ch, 1 dc in same sp as last sc (1 ch-2 sp inc'd at each side). Ch 1, turn.

Row 21 1 sc in first dc, *5 dc in next sc, 1 sc in next ch-5 sp, 1 sc in 3rd of next 5 dc, 5 dc in next sc, 1 sc in 3rd of next 5 dc, 5 dc in next sc, 1 sc in next ch-5 sp; rep from *, end 5 dc in next sc, 1 sc in last ch-5 sp. Ch 5, turn.

Row 22 and 23 Rep rows 2 and 3.

Row 24 2 dc in first sc, *1 sc in next ch-5 sp, 5 dc in next sc, 1 sc in 3rd of next 5 dc, ch 5, 1 sc in next ch-5 sp, ch 5, 1 sc in 3rd of next 5 dc, 5 dc in next sc; rep from, end 1 sc in next ch-5 sp, 3 dc in last sc. Ch 1, turn.

Row 25 1 sc in first dc, *5 dc in next sc, 1 sc in 3rd of next 5 dc, ch 5, 1 sc in next ch-5 sp, 5 dc in next sc, 1 sc in next ch-5 sp, ch 5, 1 sc in 3rd of next 5 dc; rep from *, end 5 dc in next sc, 1 sc

in top of t-ch. Ch 5, turn.

Rows 2-25 set diamond pat and incs for sleeves.

BACK

Ch 70 (86, 102) loosely. Work in diamond pat for back and front, working rows 1-9 once, then rows 2-9 eight times more, then rows 2-5 once more, ending with a RS row. Piece measures approx 26½"/67cm from beg.

Next row 1 sc in 3rd of next 5 dc, *ch 3, loosely, 1 sc in next ch-5 sp, ch 3 loosely, 1 sc in 3rd in of next 5 dc; rep from*, end ch 2, 1 sc in last sc. Fasten off.

FRONT

Ch 70 (86, 102) loosely. Work in diamond pat for back and front, working row 1-9 once, then rows 2-9 seven times more, ending with a RS row.

Neck shaping

Next row (WS) [1sc in 3rd of next 5 dc, ch 5, 1 sc in next ch-5 sp, 5 dc in next sc, 1 sc in 3rd of next 5 dc, 5 dc in the next sc, 1 sc in next ch-5 sp, ch 5] 1 (1, 2) times, 1 sc in 3rd of next 5 dc, [2 ch, 1 dc in next sc] 1 (0, 1) time, [ch 5, 1 sc in next ch-5 sp, 5 dc in next sc, 1 sc in 3rd of next 5 dc, 3 dc in next sc] 0 (1, 0) time. Ch 1 turn.

Next row 1 sc in first dc, [ch 5, 1 sc in 3rd of next 5 dc, 5 dc in next sc, 1 sc in next ch-5 sp] 0 (1, 0) time, [ch 5, 1 sc in next ch-5 sp, 5 dc in next sc, 1 sc in 3rd of next 5 dc, ch 5, 1 sc in 3rd of next 5 dc, 5 dc in next sc, 1 sc in next ch-5 sp] 1 (1, 2) times, ch 5, 1 sc in t-ch. Ch 3, turn.

Cont on these sts for first side of neck and work a further 10 rows in diamond pat, ending with row 5.

Next row 1 sc in 3rd of next 5 dc, [ch 3 loosely, 1 sc in next ch-5 sp, ch 3 loosely, 1 sc in 3rd of next 5 sc] 2 (3, 4) times, ch 2 loosely, 1 sc next sc. Fasten off.

With WS facing, rejoin yarn to top of last dc worked on inside edge of first row of neck shaping, ch 3, 1 sc in next ch-5 sp, [ch 3 loosely, 1 sc in 3rd of next 5 dc, ch 3 loosely, 1 sc in next ch-5 sp] 3 times, ch 3, work 1 (3, 1) dc in next sc, [ch 2, 1 sc in 3rd of next 5 dc, ch 5, 1 sc in next ch-5 sp, 5 dc in next sc] 1 (0,1) time, [1 sc in 3rd of next 5 dc, 5 dc in next sc, 1 sc in next ch-5 sp, ch 5, 1 sc in 3rd of next 5 dc, ch 5, 1 sc in next ch-5 sp, 5 dc in next sc] 0 (1, 1) time, 1 sc in 3rd of next 5 dc, 5 dc in next sc, 1 sc in next ch-5 sp, ch 5, 1 sc in 3rd of next 5 ch, ch 2, 1 dc in last sc. Ch 1, turn.

Next row 1 sc in first dc, [ch 5, 1 sc in next ch-5 sp, 5 dc in next sc, 1 sc in 3rd of next 5 dc, ch 5, 1 sc in 3rd of next 5 dc, 5 dc in next sc, 1 sc in next ch-5 sp] 1 (1, 2) times, ch 5, [1 sc in next dc] 1 (0, 1) time, [1sc in next ch-5 sp, 5 dc in next sc, 1 sc in 3rd of next 5 dc, ch 5, 1 sc in 3rd of next 3 dc] 0 (1, 0) time. Ch 3 (5, 3), turn. Cont on these sts for second side of neck and work a further 10 rows in diamond pat, ending with row 5.

Next row 1 sc in 3rd of next 5 dc, [ch 3 loosely, 1 sc in next ch-5 sp, ch 3 loosely, 1 sc in next 5 sc] 2 (3, 4) times, ch 2 loosely, 1 sc in next sc. Fasten off.

SLEEVES

Ch 38 loosely. Work rows 1-25 in diamond pat for sleeves, increasing on rows 4, 8, 16 and 20 as indicated. Keeping pat correct as set and working inc of 1 half dc group or 1 ch-2 sp at each side as appropriate, work a further 25 rows in diamond pat, inc at each side of pat rows 4, 8, 16 and 20 (last row worked will be as row 2 of diamond pat for sleeves).

Next row 1 sc in first dc, ch 3 loosely, 1 sc in next ch-5 sp, *[ch 3 loosely, 1 sc in 3rd of next 5 dc] twice, [ch 3 loosely, 1 sc in next ch-5 sp] twice; rep from * to end—69 sts. Fasten off.

FINISHING

Block pieces to measurements. Sew shoulder seams.

Neck edging

With RS facing, rejoin yarn at inside edge of left shoulder seam, ch 1, work 1 sc in same place, work 17 sc evenly down left side of front neck, 1 sc in first sc at front neck, [1 sc in each of next 3 ch, 1 sc in next sc] 6 times, 17 sc evenly up right side of front neck, then work across back neck sts as foll: 1 sc in next sc, [1 sc in each of next 3 ch, 1 sc in next sc] 6 times, sl st to first sc of rnd—85 sc.

Next rnd Ch 3, 2 dc in same place as last sl st, skip 2 sc, [1 sc in next sc, skip 1 sc, 5 dc in next sc, skip 1 sc] 3 times, 1 sc in next sc, skip 2 sc, 5 dc in next sc, skip 1 sc, [1 sc in next sc, skip 1 sc, 5 dc in next sc, skip 1 sc] 5 times, 1 sc in next sc, skip 1 sc, 5 dc in next sc, skip 2 dc, [1 sc in next sc, skip 1 sc, 5 dc in next sc, skip 1 sc] 3 times, 1 sc in next sc, skip 2 dc, [5 dc in next sc, skip 1 sc, 1 sc in next sc, skip 1 sc] 6 times, skip 1 sc, 2 dc in same sc as first ch-3 and 2 dc, sl st in top of ch-3. Fasten off.

Shell edging for back and front

With WS facing and working along other side of base ch at lower edge of back, rejoin yarn in first ch, 1 sc in same ch, 1 sc in each ch to end— 69 (85, 101) sc. Ch 1, turn.

Next row 1 sc in first sc, *skip 1 sc, 5 dc in next sc, skip 1 sc, 1 sc in next sc; rep from * to end. Fasten off.

Rep along lower edge of front.

Shell edging for sleeves

Work as for shell edging for back.

Place markers 9"/23cm down from shoulder seams on back and front for armholes. Sew top of sleeves between markers. Sew side and sleeve seams.

Make one 60"/150cm length ch and pull through neck edge for decorative cord.

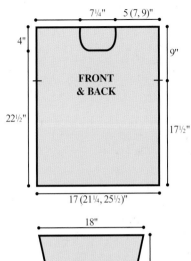

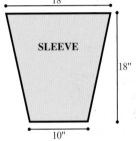

Modern Classic

for beginner knitters

Mari Lynn Patrick's buttonless jacket, knit in one piece, offers comfort for days of reflection and relaxation. Add a separate collar and garter stitch edging for subtle accent. "Modern Classic" first appeared in the Winter '98/'99 issue of *Family Circle Easy Knitting* magazine.

MATERIALS

- *Lamb's Pride Bulky* by Brown Sheep, 4oz/113g skeins, each approx 125yd/114m (wool/mohair)
  8 (9, 9, 10, 10, 11) skeins #M23 fuchsia
- One pair size 10 (6mm) straight needles
- One size 10$\frac{1}{2}$ (7mm) circular needle, 36"/90cm long
- 2yd/1.85m of 1"/2.5cm grosgrain ribbon and thread to match

SIZES

Sized for Small (Medium, Large, X-Large, XX-Large, XXX-Large). Shown in size Large.

FINISHED MEASUREMENTS

- Bust (closed) 43 (45, 47$\frac{1}{2}$, 49$\frac{1}{2}$, 52, 54$\frac{1}{2}$)"/109 (114, 120.5, 125.5, 132, 138.5)cm
- Length 27$\frac{3}{4}$ (28$\frac{1}{2}$, 29$\frac{1}{4}$, 30, 31, 31$\frac{1}{4}$)"/70.5 (72.5, 74.5, 76, 78.5, 79.5)cm
- Upper arm 16 (17, 17$\frac{1}{2}$, 19$\frac{1}{4}$, 20, 21)"/40.5 (43, 44.5, 49, 50.5, 53)cm

GAUGE

14 sts and 20 rows to 4"/10cm over St st using larger needle.
TAKE TIME TO CHECK YOUR GAUGE

Note

Cardigan is made all in one piece, beg at lower edge of back and ending at lower edge of fronts.

BACK

With smaller needles cast on 74 (78, 82, 86, 90, 94) sts. K 2 rows for hem. Change to larger circular needle and work back and forth as with straight needles as foll:

Row 1 (RS) Knit.
Row 2 K2 (selvage sts), p to last 2 sts, k2 (selvage sts). Rep these 2 rows until piece measures 19$\frac{1}{2}$ (20, 20$\frac{1}{2}$, 20$\frac{1}{2}$, 21, 21)"/49.5 (50.5, 52, 52, 53, 53) cm from beg, end with a WS row.

Beg sleeves

Cont to work the k2 garter sts in the same place (for armhole detail as in photo), AT SAME TIME, cast on 6 sts at beg of next 14 (18, 20, 4, 0, 0) rows, 5 sts at beg of next 6 (2, 0, 20, 24, 24) rows—188 (196, 202, 210, 210, 214) sts.
Next row (RS) Knit.
Next row (WS) K2 (sleeve cuff trim), [p to sleeve detail, k2] twice, p to last 2 sts, k2 (sleeve cuff trim). Work even on all sts until there are 20 (22, 24, 24, 26, 28) rows in sleeve cuff and sleeve cuff measures 4 (4$\frac{1}{2}$, 4$\frac{3}{4}$, 4$\frac{3}{4}$, 5$\frac{1}{4}$, 5$\frac{1}{2}$)"/10 (11.5, 12, 12, 13.5, 14)cm. End with a WS row. This completes back and half of sleeves.

Beg left front

Next row (RS) Work 84 (87, 90, 94, 94, 95) sts and sl to a holder to be worked later for right front, bind off center 20 (22, 22, 22, 22, 24) sts for neck and work to end. Work 3 rows even on these 84 (87, 90, 94, 94, 95) sts for left front.
Next row (RS) Inc 1 st at beg of row (neck edge), work to end. Cont to inc 1 st at neck edge every other row 3 times more, then cast on 2 sts at neck edge every other row twice, cast on 3 sts once, cast on 3 (4, 4, 4, 4. 5) sts once—98 (102, 105, 109, 109, 111) sts.
Next row (WS) Work as established to last 4 sts, k4.

Next row (RS) K3, p1 (for front band), work established pat to end. Cont to work in this way until there are a total of 40 (44, 48, 48, 52, 56) rows in sleeve cuff and sleeve cuff measures 8 (9, 9$\frac{1}{2}$, 9$\frac{1}{2}$, 10$\frac{1}{2}$, 11)"/20.5 (23, 24, 24, 26.5, 28)cm, end with a RS row. Corresponding to cast-ons, bind off from sleeve cuff edge, 5 sts 3 (1, 0, 10, 12, 12) times, 6 sts 7 (9, 10, 2, 0, 0) times—41 (43, 45, 47, 49, 51) sts. Cont to work k2 salvage sts and front band detail as before, work even until there are same number of rows as back. Change to smaller needles, k2 rows and bind off.

RIGHT FRONT

Work to correspond to left front, reversing shaping and detail placements.

FINISHING

Block pieces to measurements. Turn lower edges of hems (along ridge) on fronts and back to WS and sew in place. Sew side and sleeve seams.

Collar

Note

Collar is picked up and knit around shaped neck edge in st increments at ends of rows until all sts are picked up to front bands.

(Continued on page 135)

Night Light
for intermediate crocheters

Easy-to-crochet medallions make up this sexy evening wrap for a tasteful touch of shine. You stitch the first medallion, and then join subsequent ones to the last row. Sew on scads of shimmering sequins. "Night Light" first appeared in the Holiday '02 issue of *Family Circle Easy Knitting* magazine.

MATERIALS

▪ *Fiora* by Adrienne Vittadini Yarns, .88oz/25g balls, each approx 52yd/48m (mohair/nylon/wool/polyester)
 9 balls in #31 plum
▪ Size J/10 (6mm) crochet hook OR SIZE TO OBTAIN GAUGE

FINISHED MEASUREMENTS

▪ 18" x 39"/45.5 x 99cm

GAUGE

One medallion to 9"/23cm using size J/10 (6mm) crochet hook.
TAKE TIME TO CHECK YOUR GAUGE.

MEDALLION A

Ch 8. Join ch with a sl st forming a ring. **Rnd 1** Ch 3 (counts as 1 dc), work 23 dc in ring. Join rnd with a sl st in 3rd ch of ch-3. **Rnd 2** Ch 5 (counts as 1 dc and ch 2), sk first st, *dc in next st, ch 2, sk next st; rep from * around 11 times. Join rnd with a sl st in 3rd ch of ch-5—12 ch-2 sps. **Rnd 3** Ch 4 (counts as 1 tr), work 3 tr in first ch-2 sp, *work 4 tr in next ch-2 sp; rep from * around 11 times. Join rnd with a sl st in 4th ch of ch-4. **Rnd 4** Ch 3 (counts as 1 dc), [yo, draw up a lp in next st, yo and draw through 2 lps on hook] 3 times, yo and draw through all 4 lps on hook, ch 6, *dc in next st, [yo, draw up a lp in next st, yo and draw through 2 lps on hook] 3 times, yo and draw through all 4 lps on hook, ch 6; rep from * around 11 times. Join rnd with a sl st in 3rd ch of ch-3—12 ch-6 lps. **Rnd 5** Ch 1 (counts as 1 sc), work 3 sc in first ch-6 lp, ch 3, sl st in last sc made (picot made), work 4 sc in same ch-6 lp, *work 4 sc in next ch-6 lp, ch 3, sl st in last sc made, work 4 sc in same ch-6 lp; rep from * around 11 times. Join rnd with a sl st in first ch of ch-1. Fasten off.

MEDALLION B

(make 14)

Work as for medallion A to rnd 5. **Rnd 5 (joining)** Ch 1 (counts as 1 sc), work 3 sc in first ch-6 lp, ch 3, sl st in last sc made (picot made), work 4 sc in same ch-6 lp, * work 4 sc in next ch-6 lp, ch 3, sl st in last sc made, work 4 sc in same ch-6 lp; rep from * around 9 times, end [work 4 sc in next ch-6 lp, ch 1, sc in picot of medallion A (joining st), ch 1, work 4 sc in same ch-6 lp] twice. Join rnd with a sl st in first ch of ch-1. Fasten off.

Referring to medallion placement diagram, join next medallion B (on rnd 5) to medallion A and to first medallion B, working picot sts and joining sts wherever needed. Cont to join 12 rem medallions together following diagram.

FINISHING

Lightly block piece to measurements.

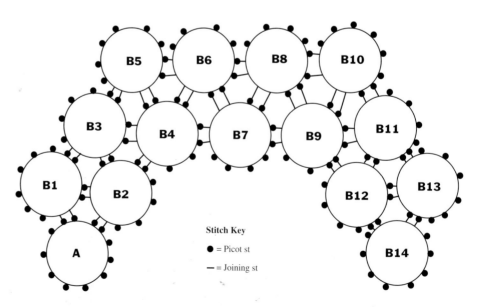

Stitch Key

● = Picot st

— = Joining st

Take it Easy

for beginner crocheters

Everyone deserves a little downtime. Jacqueline Van Dillen's lush openwork shawl requires very little effort and is a cozy comfort at the end of a long day. "Take it Easy" first appeared in the Winter '02/'03 issue of *Family Circle Easy Knitting* magazine.

MATERIALS
▓ *Tundra Ondé* by DiVé/LBUSA, $1^3/_4$oz/50g balls, each approx 55yd/75m (wool/acrylic)
   17 balls in #467 grey tweed
▓ Size K/$10^1/_2$ (6.5mm) crochet hook OR SIZE TO OBTAIN GAUGE

FINISHED MEASUREMENTS
▓ Approx 33" x 55"/84cm xm 140cm

GAUGE
5 mesh (ch 3, sc) to $5^1/_2$"/14cm and 10 rows to 4"/10cm over pat st using size K/$10^1/_2$ (6.5mm) crochet hook.
TAKE TIME TO CHECK YOUR GAUGE.

PATTERN STITCH
(multiple of 3 sts)
Row 1 Work 1 sc in 3rd ch from hook *ch 3, sk 2 sc, sc in next ch; rep from *, end with a sc in last ch.

Row 2 *Ch 3, sc in next ch-3 sp; rep from *, end sc in last ch-3.
Rep row 2 for pat st.

SHAWL
Ch 144. Work in pat st until piece measures 55"/140cm. Fasten off.

FINISHING
With RS facing, work 1 rnd sc evenly around outside edge of shawl.

Summer Sensations

Lighten up with cool stitches and chic, sleek silhouettes.

Light and Lacy

for advanced crocheters

Challenge your skills with this breezy square-necked pullover. Set-in sleeves, subtle shaping and a lacy stitchwork add up to one great looking garment. "Light and Lacy" first appeared in the Spring/Summer '01 issue of *Family Circle Easy Knitting* magazine.

MATERIALS

- *Knit-Cro-Sheen* by J & P Coats®, 1.43oz/1.32g balls, each approx 225yd/205m (cotton) 10 (12) balls in #001 white
- Size B/1 (2mm) crochet hook

SIZES

Sized for Small/Medium (Large). Shown in size Medium.

FINISHED MEASUREMENTS

- Bust 40 (46)"/101.5 (117)cm
- Length 25$\frac{1}{2}$ (28$\frac{1}{2}$)"/64.5 (72.5)cm
- Upper arm 17$\frac{1}{2}$ (21)"/44.5 (53.5)cm

GAUGE

1 rep to 3$\frac{1}{2}$"/9cm and 10 rows to 4"/10cm over chart pat using size B/1 (2mm) crochet hook. TAKE TIME TO CHECK YOUR GAUGE.

BACK

Ch 167 (197). Work in chart pat, working 30-st rep 5 (6) times. Work rows 1-18 once, then cont to rep rows 3-18 until piece measures 25$\frac{1}{2}$ (28$\frac{1}{2}$)"/64.5 (72.5)cm from beg.

FRONT

Work as for back until piece measures 22$\frac{1}{2}$ (24$\frac{1}{2}$)"/57 (65)cm rom beg, end with a chart row 9 (17).

Neck shaping

Leave center 2 motifs unworked for neck, and working both sides at once, cont in pat, beg with row 9 of chart 2 for placement of pat, until same length as back. Fasten off sts each side.

SLEEVES

Ch 77. Work in chart pat, beg with row 1 (9), and work 30-st rep twice. Cont as established until 13 rows have been worked from beg, then inc clusters and leaf motif pats each side over next 13 rows until you have one extra full motif each side. After 2 full row reps of chart pat have been worked, cont inc motifs each side until there are 5 (6) motifs in total. Work even until there are 49 rows from beg—piece measures approx 19"/48cm from beg. Fasten off.

FINISHING

Block pieces to measurements. Sew shoulder seams. Place markers 8$\frac{3}{4}$ (10$\frac{1}{2}$)"/22.5 (26.5)cm down from shoulder seams on front and back for armholes. Sew top of sleeve between markers. Sew side and sleeve seams.

(See charts on page 131)

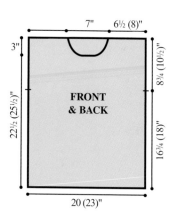

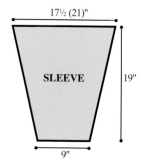

Cape Crusader

for beginner crocheters

Featuring a winsome scallop pattern and a crochet flower at the center front, Shirley Paden's enchanting capelet lends a romantic note to any summer ensemble. "Cape Crusader" first appeared in the Spring/Summer '02 issue of *Family Circle Easy Knitting* magazine.

MATERIALS

- *Grace* by Patons®, 1³/₄oz/50g balls, each approx 136yd/125m (cotton)
  3 balls in #6005 white
- Size D/3 (3.25mm) crochet hook OR SIZE TO OBTAIN GAUGE
- One safety pin
- One ¹/₄"/6mm pearl ball button

SIZE
One size.

FINISHED MEASUREMENTS

- Neck 21"/53cm
- Length 8"/20cm
- Lower edge 44"/112cm

GAUGE
24 sts and 28 rows to 4"/10cm over sc using size D/3 (3.25mm) crochet hook.
TAKE TIME TO CHECK YOUR GAUGE.

CAPELET
Beg at neck edge, ch 133.

Foundation row Sc in 2nd ch from hook and in each ch across—132 sts. Ch 1, turn.

Row 1(RS) Sc in first 5 sts, *ch 4, sk next 2 sts, sc in next st; rep from * across, end sc in last 4 sts—41 ch-4 lps. Ch 1, turn.

Rows 2-4 Sc in first 5 sts, *ch 4, sc in next ch-4 lp; rep from * across, end sc in last 5 sts. Ch 1, turn.

Row 5 Sc in first 5 sts, *ch 5, sc in ch-4 lp; rep from * across, end sc in last 5 sts. Ch 1, turn.

Rows 6-8 Sc in first 5 sts, *ch 5, sc in ch-5 lp; rep from * across, end sc in last 5 sts. Ch 1, turn.

Row 9 Sc in first 5 sts, *ch 6, sc in ch-5 lp; rep from * across, end sc in last 5 sts. Ch 1, turn.

Row 10 (WS) Sc in first 5 sts, *ch 6, sc in ch-6 lp; rep from * across, end sc in last 5 sts.

Joining
Taking care not to twist work, join piece with a sl st in first sc forming a circle. Ch 1, turn. Work now in the round.

Rnd 11 Sc in first 5 sts, *ch 6, sc in ch-6 lp; rep from * around, end ch 6, do not work across last 5 sc.

Rnds 12-14 Sc in first 10 sc (front placket), *ch 6, sc in ch-6 lp; rep from * around, end ch 6.

Rnd 15 Sc in first st of front placket, ch 7, sk next 3 sts, sc in next st (mark this ch-7 lp just made with the safety pin to indicate beg of rnd), ch 7, sk next 4 sts, sc in next st, *ch 7, sc in ch-6 lp; rep from * around. Mark first lp made of each remaining rnds with the safety pin.

Rnds 16-20 *Ch 7, sc in ch-7 lp; rep from * around.

Rnd 21 *Ch 8, sc in ch-7 lp; rep from * around.

Rnds 22-25 *Ch 8, sc in ch-8 lp; rep from * around. When rnd 25 is completed, join rnd with a sl st in first ch-8 lp of last rnd. Fasten off.

FINISHING

Neck Edging
From RS, join yarn with a sl st at base of right neck opening, ch 1.

Row 1 Making sure that work lies flat, sc evenly along entire neck edge, working 3 sc in each corner. Ch 2, do not turn.

Row 2 Working from left to right, sk first st, *sc in next st, ch 2, sk next st; rep from * across, end sc in last st. Fasten off.

Florette
Foundation ring Ch 6 leaving a long tail for sewing. Join ch with a sl st forming a ring.

Rnd 1 Ch 3, *make popcorn: work 5 dc over ring. Remove hook from working lp, then insert hook under top 2 loops of first dc. Place working loop back onto hook. Yo, and draw through all lps on hook. Pull lead yarn to gather sts tog. Ch 3; rep from * around 5 times more. Join rnd with a sl st in 3rd ch of ch-3.

Rnd 2 Ch 1, *sc in 3rd st of popcorn, ch 3, sc in ch-3 lp, ch 3; rep from * around 5 times more. Join rnd with a sl st in ch-1. Fasten off. Turn to WS of florette. Thread tail of foundation ring into tapestry needle. To close hole in center, run needle under base of dc sts. Pull tail to close opening. Fasten off securely on WS. Sew pearl button to center of florette. Sew florette to base of neck opening, as shown.

Sweet Treat

for beginner crocheters

Splash some color into your closet. Alternating rows of single and double crochet shape up this luscious cardigan designed by Gail Diven. "Sweet Treat" first appeared in the Spring/Summer '98 issue of *Family Circle Easy Knitting* magazine.

MATERIALS

- *Wintuk* by Caron International, 3½oz/100g skeins, each approx 213yd/196m (acrylic) 6 (6, 6, 7) skeins in #3094 lilac
- Size H/8 (5mm) crochet hook
- Five ⅝"/16mm buttons

SIZES

Sized for X-Small (Small, Medium, Large).
Shown in size X-Small.

FINISHED MEASUREMENTS

- Bust 34½ (37, 38, 40½)"/87.5 (94, 96.5, 102.5)cm
- Waist 32 (34½, 36, 38)"/81 (87.5, 91.5, 96.5)cm
- Length 19¼ (19¼, 21, 21)"/49 (49, 54, 54)cm
- Upper arm 13½ (14, 14¾, 15½)"/34 (35.5, 37, 38.5)cm

GAUGE

13 sts and 11 rows to 4"/10cm over pat st using size H/8 (5mm) hook.
TAKE TIME TO CHECK YOUR GAUGE.

Note

All sc, hdc and dc are referred to as sts.

BACK

Ch 58 (62, 64, 68). **Row 1 (RS)** Dc in 4th ch from hook and in each ch to end—56 (60, 62, 66) sts. Turn on this and all foll rows. **Row 2** Ch 1, sc in each st to end. **Row 3** Ch 3 (counts as 1 dc), dc in each st to end. Rep rows 2 and 3 for pat st 3 times more. **Dec row 10 (WS):** Ch 1, skip first st, sc to last 2 sts, skip next st, sc in top of t-ch. **Row 11** Rep row 3. **Row 12** Rep dec row 10—52 (56, 58, 62) sts. Work even in pat for 7 more rows. **Inc row 20 (WS):** Work 2 sc in first st, work to last 2 sts, work 2 sc in next st, sc in top of t-ch. Work 3 rows even. **Row 24** Rep inc row 20—56 (60, 62, 66) sts. Work even in pat st until there are 32 (32, 34, 34) rows from beg. Piece measures approx 11½ (11½, 12½, 12½)"/29 (29, 32, 32) cm from beg.

Armhole shaping

Row 1 (RS) Do not ch, sl st in first 4 (5, 4, 5) sts, hdc in next st, dc to last 5 (6, 5, 6) sts, hdc in next st, leave rem 4 (5, 4, 5) sts unworked. **Row 2 (WS)** Ch 1, skip first st, sc to last st, leave this st unworked—46 (48, 52, 54) sts. Work even in pat until there are 20 (20, 22, 22) rows and armhole measures 7¼ (7¼, 8, 8)"/18.5 (18.5, 20.5, 20.5)cm.

Shoulder and neck shaping

Row 1 (RS) Do not ch, sl st across first 4 (4, 5, 5) sts, sc in next st, hdc in next st, 1 dc in each of next 7 (8, 8, 9) sts, fasten off for shoulder. Skip center 20 (20, 22, 22) sts for neck, rejoin yarn in next st and ch 3 (counts as 1 dc), dc in next 6 (7, 7, 8) sts, hdc in next st, sc in next st, leave rem sts unworked and fasten off.

LEFT FRONT

Ch 30 (32, 34, 36). Work in pat st on 28 (30, 32, 34) sts as for back for 9 rows. **Row 10 (WS)** Ch 1, sc to last 2 sts, skip next st, sc in top of t-ch. Work 1 row even. **Row 12** Rep row 10—26 (28, 30, 32) sts. Work even in pat for 7 more rows. **Row 20** Ch 1, sc to last 2 sts, work 2 sc in next st, sc in top of t-ch. Work 3 rows even. **Row 24** Rep row 20—28 (30, 32, 34) sts. Work even in pat st until there are 32 rows from beg.

Neck and armhole shaping

Note

Neck shaping for sizes Medium and Large ONLY, beg 2 rows before armholes.

Row 33 (RS) For X-Small and Small, do not ch, sl st across first 4 (5, 0, 0) sts, 1 (1, 0, 0) sc in next st, 1 (1, 0, 0) hdc in next st, then for all sizes, dc to last 2 sts, [yo and pull up a lp in next st, yo and through 2 lps on hook] twice, then yo and pull through all 3 lps on hook—1 dc dec for neck. **Row 34** Ch 1, sc to last 1 (1, 0, 0) st, leave this st unworked (for X-Small and Small only). **Row 35** For Medium and Large only, do not ch, sl st across first 0 (0, 5, 5) sts, 0 (0, 1, 1) sc in next st, 0 (0, 1, 1) hdc in next st, then for all sizes, dc to last 2 sts, work 1 dc dec. **Row 36** Ch 1, sc to last 0 (0, 1, 1) st, leave this st unworked (for Medium and Large only). Cont to work in pat, working 1 dc dec every RS row for neck until 13 (14, 15, 16) sts rem. Work 1 more WS row—there are 20 (20, 22, 22) rows in armhole. Shape shoulder as for back.

(Continued on page 133)

Easy Elegance

for intermediate crocheters

With a graceful curved neckline, allluring openwork lace pattern and a flattering silhouette, this light-as-air short-sleeved pullover takes you from day to night in comfort and style. "Easy Elegance" first appeared in the Spring/Summer '01 issue of *Family Circle Easy Knitting* magazine.

MATERIALS

- *Speed Cro-Sheen* by J & P Coats®/Coats & Clark®, 1.6oz/1.47g balls, each approx 100yd/91m (cotton)
  9 (10, 11) balls in #123 yellow
- Size E/4 (3.5mm) crochet hook

SIZES

Sized for Small (Medium, Large). Shown in size Medium.

FINISHED MEASUREMENTS

- Bust 34 (37, 40)"/86.5 (94, 101.5)cm
- Length 22¾ (23¼, 24½)"/57.5 (60, 62.5)cm
- Upper arm 14 (15½, 17)"/35.5 (39.5, 43)cm

GAUGE

2½ reps and 12½ rows to 4"/10cm over chart pat using double strand and size E/4 (3.5mm) crochet hook.
TAKE TIME TO CHECK YOUR GAUGE.

Note

Work with 2 strands held tog throughout.

BACK

Ch 120 (132, 144) plus 7 extra. Work in chart pat, working 12-st rep 10 (11, 12) times. Work rows 1-8 once, then cont to rep rows 5-8 until piece measures 15 (15½ 15¾)"/38 (39, 40)cm from beg.

Armhole shaping

Leave 1 motif unworked each side on next row, work 3 rows even, then leave ½ motif unworked each side—7 (8, 9) motifs plus edge sts. Work even until armhole measures 7¾ (8¼, 8¾)"/19.5 (21, 22.5)cm. Fasten off.

FRONT

Work as for back until piece measures 19¼ (20¼, 21)"/48.5 (51, 53.5)cm from beg.

Neck shaping

Leave center 1½ (1½, 2½) motifs unworked for neck, and working both sides at once, leave ½ motif unworked at each neck edge every other row twice. Work even until same length as back. Fasten off sts each side for shoulders.

SLEEVES

Ch 60 (60, 72) plus 7 extra. Work in chart pat, working 12-st rep 5 (5, 6) times. Work rows 1-8 once, then cont to rep rows 5-8. Cont as established inc 1½ (2, 2) motifs each side evenly over next 5½ (6, 6½)"/14 (15.5, 16.5)cm. Work even until piece measures 6 (6½, 7)"/15.5 (16.5, 17.5)cm from beg.

Cap shaping

Dec ½ motif at end of next 14 (16, 18) rows. Work even until cap measures 5 (5½, 6)"/12.5 (14, 15.5)cm. Fasten off.

FINISHING

Block pieces to measurements. Sew shoulder seams. Set in sleeves. Sew side and sleeve seams. With RS facing, work 1 row sc evenly around neck and lower edges of body and sleeves.

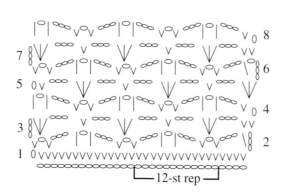

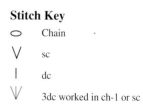

Stitch Key

◯	Chain
V	sc
I	dc
⋁	3dc worked in ch-1 or sc

Vintage Verve

for experienced crocheters

Tatyana Mirer's pineapple patterned wraps recalls gentler days gone by. Lush fringe and generous size make it the ultimate evening accessory. "Vintage Verve" first appeared in the Spring/Summer '02 issue of *Family Circle Easy Knitting* magazine.

MATERIALS

- *Isa* by Sesia/LBUSA, 1³⁄₄oz/50g balls, each approx 160yd/145m (cotton/viscose)
  13 balls in #51 white
- Size D/3 (3.25mm) crochet hook OR SIZE TO OBTAIN GAUGE

FINISHED MEASUREMENTS

- 75"/190cm wide by 40"/102cm long (not including fringe)

GAUGE

24 sts and 12 rows to 4"/10cm over dc using size D/3 (3.25mm) crochet hook.
TAKE TIME TO CHECK YOUR GAUGE.

STITCH GLOSSARY

Shell Work (2 dc, ch 2, 2 dc) in same sp. When working a shell in a shell, work in ch-2 sp of shell.

SHAWL

Beg at bottom point, ch 12. Join ch with a sl st forming a ring.

Row 1 Work 10 dc over ring, tr over ring. Ch 3, turn.

Row 2 Sk tr, [dc in next 2 sts, ch 2] 4 times, dc in last 2 sts, end tr in ch-3 turning ch. Ch 3, turn.

Row 3 [Shell in next ch-2 sp, ch 3] 3 times, work shell in last ch-2 sp, end tr in ch-3 turning ch. Ch 3, turn.

Row 4 Shell in next shell, ch 3, shell in next shell, ch 2, work 5 dc in next ch-3 sp, ch 2, shell in next shell, ch 3, shell in next shell, end tr in ch-3 turning ch. Ch 3, turn.

Row 5 [Shell in next shell, ch 3] twice, dc in next ch-2 sp, dc in next 5 sts, dc in next ch-2 sp, [ch 3, shell in next shell] twice, end tr in ch-3 turning ch. Ch 3, turn.

Row 6 [Shell in next shell, ch 3] twice, dc in next ch-3 sp, dc in next 7 sts, dc in next ch-3 sp, [ch 3, shell in next shell] twice, end tr in ch-3 turning ch. Ch 3, turn.

Row 7 [Shell in next shell, ch 3] twice, dc in next ch-3 sp, dc in next 9 sts, dc in next ch-3 sp, [ch 3, shell in next shell] twice, end tr in ch-3 turning ch. Ch 3, turn.

Row 8 [Shell in next shell, ch 3] twice, [dc in next st, ch 1] 10 times, dc in next st, [ch 3, shell in next shell] twice, end tr in ch-3 turning ch. Ch 3, turn.

Row 9 Shell in next shell, ch 3, shell in next shell, ch 4, [sc in next ch-1 sp, ch 5 (loop)] 9 times, ch 4, shell in next shell, ch 3, shell in next shell, end tr in ch-3 turning ch. Ch 3, turn.

Row 10 Shell in next shell, ch 3, shell in next shell, ch 4, [sc in next loop, ch 5] 8 times, sc in next loop, ch 4, shell in next shell, ch 3, shell in next shell, end tr in ch-3 turning ch. Ch 3, turn.

Row 11 (inc row) Shell in next shell, ch 3, work (2 dc, ch 2, 2 dc, ch 2, 2 dc) in next shell, ch 4, [sc in next loop, ch 5] 7 times, sc in next loop, ch 4, work (2dc, ch 2, 2dc, ch 2, 2dc) in next shell, ch 3, shell in next shell, end tr in ch-3 turning ch. Ch 3, turn.

Row 12 Shell in next shell, ch 3, shell in next ch-2 sp, ch 3, shell in next ch-2 sp, ch 4, [sc in next loop, ch 5] 6 times, sc in next loop, ch 4, shell in next ch-2 sp, ch 3, shell in next ch-2 sp, ch 3, shell in next shell, end tr in ch-3 turning ch. Ch 3, turn.

Row 13 Shell in next shell, ch 3, shell in next shell, ch 2, work 5 dc in next ch-3 sp, ch 2, shell in next shell, ch 4, [sc in next loop, ch 5] 5 times, sc in next loop, ch 4, shell in next shell, ch 2, work 5 dc in next ch-3 sp, ch 2, shell in next shell, ch 3, shell in next shell, end tr in ch-3 turning ch. Ch 3, turn.

Row 14 [Shell in next shell, ch 3] twice, dc in in next ch-2 sp, dc in next 5 sts, dc in next ch-2 sp, ch 3, shell in next shell, ch 4, [sc in next loop, ch 5] 4 times, sc in next loop, ch 4, shell in next shell, ch 3, dc in next ch-2 sp, dc in next 5 sts, dc in next ch-2 sp, [ch 3, shell in next shell] twice, end tr in ch-3 turning ch. Ch 3, turn.

Row 15 [Shell in next shell, ch 3] twice, dc in next ch-3 sp, dc in next 7 sts, dc in next ch-3 sp,

(Continued on page 44)

ch 3, shell in next shell, ch 4, [sc in next loop, ch 5] 3 times, sc in next loop, ch 4, shell in next shell, ch 3, dc in next ch-3 sp, dc in next 7 sts, dc in next ch-3 sp, [ch 3, shell in next shell] twice, end tr in ch-3 turning ch. Ch 3, turn.

Row 16 [Shell in next shell, ch 3] twice, dc in next ch-3 sp, dc in next 9 sts, dc in next ch-3 sp, ch 3, shell in next shell, ch 4, [sc in next loop, ch 5] twice, sc in next loop, ch 4, shell in next shell, ch 3, dc in next ch-3 sp, dc in next 9 sts, dc in next ch-3 sp, [ch 3, shell in next shell] twice, end tr in ch-3 turning ch. Ch 3, turn.

Row 17 [Shell in next shell, ch 3] twice, [dc in next st, ch 1] 10 times, dc in next st, ch 3, shell in next shell, ch 4, sc in next loop, ch 5, sc in next loop, ch 4, shell in next shell, ch 3, [dc in next st, ch 1] 10 times, dc in next st, [ch 3, shell in next shell] twice, end tr in ch-3 turning ch. Ch 3, turn.

Row 18 Shell in next shell, ch 3, shell in next shell, ch 4, [sc in next ch-1 sp, ch 5 (loop)] 9 times, sc in next ch-1sp, ch 4, shell in next shell, ch 4, sc in next loop, ch 4, shell in next shell, ch 4, [sc in next ch-1 sp, ch 5 (loop)] 9 times, sc in next ch-1sp, ch 4, shell in next shell, ch 3, shell in next shell, end tr in ch-3 turning ch. Ch 3, turn.

Row 19 Shell in next shell, ch 3, shell in next shell, ch 4, [sc in next loop, ch 5] 8 times, sc in next loop, ch 4, shell in next shell, ch 3, shell in next shell, ch 4, [sc in next loop, ch 5] 8 times, sc in next loop, ch 4, shell in next shell, ch 3, shell in next shell, end tr in ch-3 turning ch. Ch 3, turn.

Row 20 (inc row) Shell in next shell, ch 3, work (2 dc, ch 2, 2 dc, ch 2, 2 dc) in next shell, ch 4, [sc in next loop, ch 5] 7 times, sc in next loop, ch 4, shell in next shell, ch 3, shell in next shell, ch 4, [sc in next loop, ch 5] 7 times, sc in next loop, ch 4, work (2 dc, ch 2, 2 dc, ch 2, 2 dc) in next shell, ch 3, shell in next shell, end tr in ch-3 turning ch. Ch 3, turn.

Row 21 Shell in next shell, [ch 3, shell in next ch-2 sp] twice, ch 4, [sc in next loop, ch 5] 6 times, sc in next loop, ch 4, shell in next shell, ch 3, shell in next shell, ch 4, [sc in next loop, ch 5] 6 times, sc in next loop, ch 4, [shell in next ch-2 sp, ch 3] twice, shell in next shell, end tr in ch-3 turning ch. Ch 3, turn.

Row 22 Shell in next shell, ch 3, shell in next shell, ch 2, work 5 dc in next ch-3 sp, ch 2, shell in next shell, ch 4, [sc in next loop, ch 5] 5 times, sc in next loop, ch 4, shell in next shell, ch 2, work 5 dc in next ch-3 sp, ch 2, shell in next shell, ch 4, [sc in next loop, ch 5] 5 times, sc in next loop, ch 4, shell in next shell, ch 2, work 5 dc in next ch-3 sp, ch 2, shell in next shell, ch 3, shell in next shell, end tr in ch-3 turning ch. Ch 3, turn.

Row 23 [Shell in next shell, ch 3] twice, *dc in in next ch-2 sp, dc in next 5 sts, dc in next ch-2 sp, ch 3, shell in next shell, ch 4, [sc in next loop, ch 5] 4 times, sc in next loop, ch 4, shell in next shell, ch 3; rep from * across, end dc in next ch-2 sp, dc in next 5 sts, dc in next ch-2 sp, [ch 3, shell in next shell] twice, tr in ch-3 turning ch. Ch 3, turn.

Row 24 [Shell in next shell, ch 3] twice, *dc in next ch-3 sp, dc in next 7 sts, dc in next ch-3 sp, ch 3, shell in next shell, ch 4, [sc in next loop, ch 5] 3 times, sc in next loop, ch 4, shell in next shell, ch 3; rep from * across, end dc in next ch-3 sp, dc in next 7 sts, dc in next ch-3 sp, [ch 3, shell in next shell] twice, tr in ch-3 turning ch. Ch 3, turn.

Row 25 [Shell in next shell, ch 3] twice, *dc in next ch-3 sp, dc in next 9 sts, dc in next ch-3 sp, ch 3, shell in next shell, ch 4, [sc in next loop, ch 5] twice, sc in next loop, ch 4, shell in next shell, ch 3; rep from * across, end dc in next ch-3 sp, dc in next 9 sts, dc in next ch-3 sp, [ch 3, shell in next shell] twice, tr in ch-3 turning ch. Ch 3, turn.

Row 26 [Shell in next shell, ch 3] twice, *[dc in next st, ch 1] 10 times, dc in next st, ch 3, shell in next shell, ch 4, sc in next loop, ch 5, sc in next loop, ch 4, shell in next shell, ch 3; rep from * across, end [dc in next st, ch 1] 10 times, dc in next st, [ch 3, shell in next shell] twice, tr in ch-3 turning ch. Ch 3, turn.

Row 27 Shell in next shell, ch 3, shell in next shell, ch 4, *[sc in next ch-1 sp, ch 5 (loop)] 9 times, sc in next ch-1sp, ch 4, shell in next shell, ch 4, sc in next loop, ch 4, shell in next shell, ch 4; rep from * across, end [sc in next ch-1 sp, ch 5 (loop)] 9 times, sc in next ch-1sp, ch 4, shell in next shell, ch 3, shell in next shell, tr in ch-3 turning ch. Ch 3, turn.

Row 28 Shell in next shell, ch 3, shell in next shell, ch 4, *[sc in next loop, ch 5] 8 times, sc in next loop, ch 4, shell in next shell, ch 3, shell in next shell, ch 4; rep from * across, end [sc in next loop, ch 5] 8 times, sc in next loop, ch 4, shell in next shell, ch 3, shell in next shell, tr in ch-3 turning ch. Ch 3, turn.

Row 29 (inc row) Shell in next shell, ch 3, work (2 dc, ch 2, 2 dc, ch 2, 2 dc) in next shell, ch 4, *[sc in next loop, ch 5] 7 times, sc in next loop, ch 4, shell in next shell, ch 3, shell in next shell, ch 4; rep from * across, end [sc in next loop, ch 5] 7 times, sc in next loop, ch 4, work (2 dc, ch 2, 2 dc, ch 2, 2 dc) in next shell, ch 3, shell in next shell, tr in ch-3 turning ch. Ch 3, turn.

Row 30 Shell in next shell, [ch 3, shell in next ch-2 sp] twice, ch 4, *[sc in next loop, ch 5] 6 times, sc in next loop, ch 4, shell in next shell, ch 3, shell in next shell, ch 4; rep from * across, end [sc in next loop, ch 5] 6 times, sc in next loop, ch 4, [shell in next ch-2 sp, ch 3] twice, shell in next shell, tr in ch-3 turning ch. Ch 3, turn.

Row 31 Shell in next shell, ch 3, shell in next shell, *ch 2, work 5 dc in next ch-3 sp, ch 2, shell in next shell, ch 4, [sc in next loop, ch 5] 5 times, sc in next loop, ch 4, shell in next shell; rep from * across, end ch 2, work 5 dc in next ch-3 sp, ch 2, shell in next shell, ch 3, shell in next shell, tr in ch-3 turning ch. Ch 3, turn.

Rep rows 23-31 until there are 11 pineapple motifs across, end on row 26.

Next row (Shell in next shell, ch 3) twice, *[dc in next ch-1 sp, ch 1] 9 times, dc in next ch-1 sp, ch 3, shell in next shell, ch 4, sc in next loop, ch 4, shell in next shell, ch 3; rep from * across, end [dc in next ch-1 sp, ch 1] 9 times, dc in next ch-1 sp, [ch 3, shell in next shell] twice, tr in ch-3 turning ch. Ch 3, turn.

Following row (Shell in next shell, ch 3) twice, *[dc in next ch-1 sp, ch 1] 8 times, dc in next ch-1 sp, ch 3, [shell in next shell, ch 3] twice; rep from * across, end [dc in next ch-1 sp, ch 1] 8 times, dc in next ch-1 sp, [ch 3, shell in next shell] twice, tr in ch-3 turning ch. Ch 2, turn.

Last row *Sc in next shell, ch 1, dc in 4th dc of same shell, ch 1, dc in next ch-3 sp, ch 1, dc in first dc of next shell, ch 1, sc in same shell, ch 1, sc in next ch-3 sp, ch 1, [sc in next ch-1 sp, ch 1] 8 times, sc in next ch-3 sp, ch 1; rep from * aross, end sc in next shell, ch 1, dc in 4th dc of same shell, ch 1, dc in next ch-3 sp, ch 1, dc in first dc of next shell, ch 1, sc in same shell, ch 1, sc in ch-3 turning ch. Fasten off.

FINISHING

Block lightly.

FRINGE

In ch at bottom point and in each t-ch along side edges, attach 6 strands of yarn (each approx 13"/33cm long) held tog for each fringe.

Think Tank

for beginner crocheters

Mari Lynn Patrick's sporty mesh top brings crochet up to speed for summer. Clever keyhole neck and contrast trim keep things interesting. "Think Tank" first appeared in the Spring/Summer '98 issue of *Family Circle Easy Knitting* magazine.

MATERIALS

- *Cotton-Ease* by Lion Brand Yarn Co., 3.5oz/100g skeins, each approx 207yd/191m (cotton/acrylic)
  3 (4, 4, 5, 5) skeins in #107 candy blue (MC)
  1 skein in #100 white (CC)
- One each sizes C/2 and D/3 (2.5 and 3mm) crochet hooks OR SIZE TO OBTAIN GAUGE

SIZES

Sized for X-Small (Small, Medium, Large, X-Large). Shown in size Small.

FINISHED MEASUREMENTS

- Bust 33 (35, 37, 39, 41)"/83.5 (88, 94, 99, 104)cm
- Length 18 (18, 18½, 19, 19½)"/45.5 (45.5, 47, 48.5, 49.5)cm

GAUGE

12 mesh sps and 10 mesh rows to 4"/10cm over mesh pat using size D/3 (3mm) hook. TAKE TIME TO CHECK YOUR GAUGE.

Note

One mesh sp worked each side will be worked as a selvage (to be turned under when seaming).

BACK

With size D/3 (3mm) crochet hook and MC, ch 97 (103, 109, 115, 121).

Row 1 (RS) 1 dc in 5th ch from hook, *ch 1, skip 1 ch, 1 dc in next ch; rep from * to end—47 (50, 53, 56, 59) mesh sps, turn.

Row 2 Ch 5, *1 dc in next dc, ch 1; rep from *, end 1 dc in top of t-ch, turn. Rep row 2 for mesh pat until piece measures approx 3"/7.5cm from beg. (There are 7 mesh rows). This marks end of side slit. **Next row** Ch 7, 1 dc in 5th ch from hook, 1 dc in first ch-1 sp (2 mesh inc), *ch 1, 1 dc in next dc; rep from * to last sp, end [ch 1, 1 dc in last ch-1 sp] twice (2 mesh inc), ch 1, 1 dc in top of t-ch—51 (54, 57, 60, 63) mesh sps, turn. Work even in mesh pat until piece measures 10½"/26.5cm from beg.

Armhole shaping

Next row Ch 1, sl st in first dc, [sl st in next ch 1-sp and in next dc] 4 (4, 4, 5, 5) times, ch 5, 1 dc in next dc, cont in mesh pat to last 4 (4, 4, 5, 5) mesh sps and leave these sps unworked—4 (4, 4, 5, 5) mesh sps dec at each end of row, turn. Cont to dec 2 mesh sps at each end of next 1 (2, 2, 2, 2) rows, then dec 1 mesh sp at each end of next 2 (1, 2, 2, 3) rows—35 (36, 37, 38, 39) mesh sps. Work even until armhole measures 6½ (6½, 7, 7½, 8)"/16.5 (16.5, 17.5, 19, 20.5)cm.

Neck and shoulder shaping

Next row Work 10 (10, 10, 11, 11) mesh sps, leave center 15 (16, 17, 16, 17) sps unworked (for neck), rejoin 2nd skein MC to work last 10 (10, 10, 11, 11) mesh sps. Cont to work both sides at once with separate skeins of yarn, dec 5 sts from each neck edge once and AT SAME TIME, when armhole measures 7 (7, 7½, 8, 8½)"/17.5 (17.5, 19, 20.5, 21.5)cm, shape shoulders each side by dec 3 sts each side once, then 2 (2, 2, 3, 3) sts once.

FRONT

Work as for back until armhole measures 2 (2, 2½, 3, 3½)"/5 (5, 6.5, 7.5, 9)cm.

Neck opening

Next row Work 17 (17, 18, 18, 19) mesh sps, leave center 1 (2, 1, 2, 1) mesh sps unworked, join 2nd skein MC and work to end. Cont to work both sides separately for 2"/5cm more.

Neck shaping

Next row—First side Work 11 (11, 12, 12, 13) mesh sps, leave rem 6 sps unworked.

Second side Leave first 6 sps unworked, rejoin MC and work rem 11 (11, 12, 12, 13) mesh sps. Cont to dec at neck edge every row in this way, dec 3 sts once, 2 sts once and 1 st 1 (1, 2, 1, 2) times—5 (5, 5, 6, 6) mesh sps. When same number of rows as back, shape shoulders as on back.

FINISHING

Block pieces. Sew shoulder seams. Sew side seams (or sl st tog) taking in 1 mesh sp for a selvage at each seam.

Edging

Working around armhole with MC and size C/2 (2.5mm) hook, work 1 rnd sc evenly around armhole edge, pulling CC through last 2 lps on hook at end of rnd. Cut MC.

Rnd 2 With CC, ch 3, work 1 dc in each sc around. Join with sl st to t-ch, fasten off leaving a long end for sewing. Fold edge in half to WS and with tapestry needle, sew front lp of each dc to corresponding sc lp in MC along edge,

(Continued on page 133)

Mesh-merizing

for experienced crocheters

Mari Lynn Patrick's wave-patterned pullover works double time as a chic swimsuit cover up or lovely layering piece for a tank and Capri's. A wide boat neck and dropped shoulders, add to the carefree look. "Mesh-merizing" first appeared in the Spring/Summer '02 issue of *Family Circle Easy Knitting* magazine.

MATERIALS

- *Frosting* by Knit one, Crochet too, 1³/₄oz/50g skeins, each approx 190yd/174m (cotton/nylon) 8 (10) skeins in #100 white
- Size E/4 (3.5mm) crochet hook OR SIZE TO OBTAIN GAUGE

SIZES

Sized for Small/Large (XX-Large/XXX-Large). Shown in size Small/Large.

FINISHED MEASUREMENTS

- Bust 43 (59)"/109 (150)cm
- Length 23¹/₂ (26¹/₂)"/59.5 (67)cm
- Upper arm 13¹/₂ (21¹/₂)"/34 (55)cm

GAUGE

12 mesh sps and 10 rows to 4"/10cm over wave pat st using size E/4 (3.5mm) crochet hook.
TAKE TIME TO CHECK YOUR GAUGE.

STITCH GLOSSARY

dtr [yo hook] 4 times, insert hook into st and pull up a lp, [yo and through 2 lps] 5 times.

WAVE PATTERN STITCH

(Ch a multiple of 48 plus 36)
Note One sp is formed by a sl st, sc, dc, tr or dtr plus ch 1.
Row 1 (RS) Sl st in 2nd ch from hook, +*[Ch 1, sk 1 ch, sl st in next ch] 5 times, [ch 1, skip 1 ch, sc in next ch] twice, [ch 1, skip 1 ch, dc in next ch] twice, [ch 1, skip 1 ch, tr in next ch] twice, [ch 1, skip 1 ch, dtr in next ch] 6 times +, [ch 1, skip 1 ch, tr in next ch] twice, [ch 1, skip 1 ch, dc in next ch] twice, [ch 1, skip 1 ch, sc in next ch] twice, ch 1, skip 1 ch, sl st in next ch; rep from *, then end by rep between +'s once. Ch 1, turn.

Row 2 Sl st in first dtr, +* [ch 1, sl st in next dtr] 5 times, [ch 1, sc in next tr] twice, [ch 1, dc in next dc] twice, [ch 1, tr in next sc] twice, [ch 1, dtr in next sl st] 6 times+, [ch 1, tr in next sc] twice, [ch 1, dc in next dc] twice, [ch 1, sc in next tr] twice, ch 1, sl st in next dtr; rep from *, then end by rep between +'s once. Ch 1, turn.
Note From this point on, all sl sts, sc, dc, tr and dtr will be called sts.
Row 3 Sc in first st, *+ ch 1, sc in next st, [ch 1, dc in next st] twice, [ch 1, tr in next st] twice, [ch 1, dtr in next st] 6 times, [ch 1, tr in next st] twice, [ch 1, dc in next st] twice, [ch 1, sc in next st] twice+, [ch 1, sl st in next st] 6 times, ch 1, sc in next st; rep from * end by rep between +'s once, ch 3 (does not count as 1 tr), turn.
Row 4 Tr in first st, *+ ch1 tr in next st, [ch 1, dc in next st] twice, [ch 1, sc in next st] twice, [ch 1, sl st in next st] 6 times, [ch 1, sc in next st] twice, [ch 1, dc in next st] twice, [ch 1, tr in next st] twice+, [ch 1, dtr in next st] 6 times, ch 1, tr in next st; rep from *, end by rep between +'s once. Ch 1, turn. Rep rows 1-4 for wave pat st. (See chart for clarification.)

BACK

Ch 132 (180) for 65 (89) sps. Work in wave pat st for a total of 58 (66) rows, ending with row 2 of wave pat st. Piece measures approx 23¹/₂ (26¹/₂)"/59.5 (67)cm from beg. Fasten off.

FRONT

Work as for back for a total of 54 (62) rows. Piece measures approx 21¹/₂ (25)"/54.5 (63.5)cm from beg, end with row 2 of wave pat st. Ch 1, turn.
Neck shaping
Left shoulder
Next (row 3) Working in pat, work 2 sc, 2 dc, 2 tr, 6 dtr, 2 tr, 2 dc, 2 sc, 1 (6) sl st, 0 (2) sc, 0 (2) dc, 0 (2) tr, 0 (1) dtr for a total of 19 (31) sts. Ch 3 (1), turn.
Next (row 4) Working in pat, work 0 (1) sl st, 0 (2) sc, 0 (2) dc, 0 (2) tr, 1 (6) dtr, 2 tr, 2 dc, 2 sc, 6 sl st, 2 sc, 2 dc, 2 tr. Ch 1, turn.
Next (row 1) Work 6 sl st, 2 sc, 2 dc, 2 tr, 6 dtr, 0 (2) tr, 0 (2) dc, 0 (2) sc, 0 (6) sl st. Ch 1 turn.
Next (row 2) Work 6 sl st. Fasten off.
Right shoulder
Rejoin yarn to work last 19 (31) sts and work as for left shoulder in reverse.

SLEEVES

Beg at top edge of sleeve, ch 84 (132) for 41 (65) sps. Work in wave pat st for 8 (4) rows.
Dec row Ch 2, skip first st and sp and work into next st (dec 1 sp), work pat row 1 to last sp, leave last sp unworked. Cont to dec 1 sp each side every 4th row 8 (9) times more—23 (45) sps. Work even for 2 (0) rows.

(Continued on page 131)

Sheer Delight

for intermediate crocheters

Bands of filigree lace lend airy sophistication to Mari Lynn Patrick's long, lean open-work dress. Make fast work of it with cool cotton yarn and an oversized crochet hook. "Sheer Delight" first appeared in the Spring/Summer '99 issue of *Family Circle Easy Knitting* magazine.

MATERIALS

- *Simply Soft* by Caron International, 3oz/90g skeins, each approx 165yd/152m (acrylic) 7 skeins in #2690 blue
- Sizes H/8 and J/10 (5 and 6mm) crochet hooks OR SIZE TO OBTAIN GAUGE

SIZES

Sized for Small/Medium.

FINISHED MEASUREMENTS

- Hem 53"/134.5cm
- Bust 35"/89cm
- Length 49"/124.5cm

GAUGE

14 dc and 8 pat rows to 4"/10cm over pat st using size J/10 (6mm) hook.
TAKE TIME TO CHECK YOUR GAUGE.

PATTERN STITCH

(Chain a multiple of 4 ch plus 2 extra)

Row 1 Sc in 2nd ch from hook, *ch 7, skip 3 ch, 1 sc in next ch; rep from * to end. Ch 6, turn.

Row 2 Sc in first ch-7 sp, *ch 3, sc in next ch 7 sp; rep from *, end ch 2, dc in last sc. Ch 6, turn.

Row 3 *Sc in next sc, ch 7; rep from *, end sc in last sc, ch 3, dc in 3rd ch of t-ch. Ch 1, turn.

Row 4 Sc in first dc, *ch 3, sc in next ch-7 sp; rep from *, end ch 3, sc in 3rd ch of t-ch. Ch 3, turn.

Row 5 Skip first sc. *3 dc in ch-3 sp, dc in next sc; rep from * to end (t-ch 3 at beg counts as 1 dc). Ch 1, turn.

Row 6 Sc in first dc, *ch 7, skip 3 dc, sc in next dc; rep from * end with sc in top of t-ch. Ch 6, turn. Rep rows 2-6 for pat st.

BACK

With size J/10 (6mm) hook, ch 94. Work in pat st on 23 pats (there are 93 dc on pat row 5) until piece measures 7¼"/18.5cm from beg, end with pat row 4 of 3rd 5-row pat rep.

Dec row 5 Skip first sc (ch-3 counts as 1 dc), 2 dc in first ch-3 sp, dc in next sc, 3 dc in next ch-3 sp, dc in next sc, 2 dc in next ch-3 sp, *dc in next sc, 3 dc in ch-3 sp; rep from * to last 3 ch-3 sps, dc in next sc, 2 dc in next ch-3 sp, dc in next sc, 3 dc in next ch-3 sp, dc in next sc, 2 dc in last ch-3 sp, dc in last sc—89 dc. (4dc dec'd). Ch 1, turn. There are now 3 dc pat row bands (or pat row 5 has been worked 3 times). Rep dec row 5 on 5th, 6th, 7th, 8th, 10th, 11th, 12th and 13th pat row band (working other pat row 5 bands even in pat). There are 57 dc and 14 pats. Work 14th pat row 5 band even.

Next (15th) pat band (inc row) Dc in first sc (inc 1), 3 dc in first ch-3 sp, dc in next sc, 4 dc in next ch-3 sp, dc in next sc, work pat row 5 to last 2 ch-3 sps, 4 dc in next ch-3 sp, dc in next sc, 4 dc in next ch-3 sp, dc in top of t-ch. There are 61dc and 15 pats. Work even through end of row 5 of 16th pat row band. Piece measures approx 42"/106.5cm from beg. Cut yarn.

Armhole shaping

Next (pat row 6) Skip first 6 dc, rejoin yarn in next dc and ch 1, sc in same dc with joining and rep from * of pat row 6 to last 6 dc, leave these dc unworked. There are 49 dc and 12 pats. Ch 6, turn. **Next (pat row 2)** Skip first ch-7sp, *sc in next ch-7sp, ch 3; rep from *, end sc in last ch-7 sp (do not ch 2 and dc in last sc). Ch 6, turn. **Next row** Work pat row 3 on 11 sps. **Next row** Work pat row 4 on 11 sps. **Next row** Rep dec row 5. There are 41 dc and 10 pats. Work even until there are a total of 18 pat row 5 bands. Then work rows 6 and 2 again. Fasten off.

FRONT

Work as for back until there are a total of 17 pat row 5 bands. There are 41 dc and 10 pats.

Neck shaping

Next (pat row 6)—First side Sc in first dc, *[ch 7, skip 3 dc, sc in next dc] 3 times, leave rem dc unworked. Ch 6, turn. **Next (pat row 2)** Skip first ch-7 sp, sc in next ch 7 sp, ch 3, sc in next ch-7 sp, ch 2, dc in last sc. Work even on 9 dc and 2 pats until same number of rows as on back. Fasten off. To work 2nd side, skip center 15 dc, rejoin yarn and ch 1, sc in same dc with joining and complete to correspond to first side.

FINISHING

Do not block. Lay pieces flat and mist lightly with water. Leave until dry. With larger crochet hook, sl st tog shoulder and side seams from WS.

Edging

With smaller crochet hook, join in one side seam of hem.

Rnd 1 Working through outer lps only, work 1

(Continued on page 133)

In Bloom

for intermediate crocheters

From seaboard to seashore, softer silhouettes are the way to go. Angela Juergen's beach-friendly cover-up—featuring whimsical floral embellishments—is guaranteed to make a splash on the beach scene. "In Bloom" first appeared in the Spring/Summer '03 issue of *Family Circle Easy Knitting* magazine.

MATERIALS

- *Grace* by Patons®, 1¾oz/50g balls, each approx 136yd/125m (cotton)
  15 (16, 18, 20) balls in #60005 white
- Size B/1 and C/2 (2 and 2.5mm) crochet hooks OR SIZE TO OBTAIN GAUGE

SIZES

Sized for Small (Medium, Large, X-Large). Shown in size Medium.

FINISHED MEASUREMENTS

- Bust 38 (42, 46, 50)"/96.5 (106.5, 117, 127)cm
- Length 26½ (27, 27½, 28)"/67 (68.5, 70, 71)cm
- Upper arm 18 (19, 20, 21)"/45.5 (48, 51, 53)cm

GAUGE

29 sts and 14 rows to 5"/12.5cm over pat st using size C/2 (2.5mm) crochet hook.
TAKE TIME TO CHECK YOUR GAUGE.

Notes

1 To dec 1 sc, work as foll: [Insert hook into next st and draw up a lp] twice, yo and draw through all 3 lps on hook.

2 To dec 1 dc, work as foll: [Yo. Insert hook into next st and draw up a lp. Yo and draw through 2 lps] twice, yo and draw through all 3 lps on hook.

STITCH GLOSSARY

V-st Work (dc, ch 1, dc) in one st.

PATTERN STITCH

(multiple of 3 sts)

Row 1 (RS) Dc in first st, *sk next 2 sts, V-st in next st; rep from *, end sk next st, dc in last st. Ch 3, turn.

Row 2 Dc in first st, *sk next dc and ch-1, V-st in next st; rep from *, end sk last st, dc in 3rd ch of t-ch. Ch 3, turn.

Rep row 2 for pat st.

BACK

With larger hook, ch 112 (124, 136, 148). **Row 1** Sc in 2nd ch from hook and in each ch across—111 (123, 135, 147) sts. Ch 1, turn. **Rows 2 and 4** Sc in each st across. Ch 3, turn. **Rows 3 and 5** Dc in each st across. Ch 1, turn. **Row 6** Sc in each st across. Ch 3, turn. Work row 1 of pat st—36 (40, 44, 48) V-sts. Beg with row 2, cont in pat st and work even until piece measures approx 25½ (26, 26½, 27)"/64.5 (66, 67, 68.5)cm from beg. Ch 3, turn.

Neck shaping—Right shoulder

Next row Work in pat st across first 8 (10, 12, 14) V-sts. Ch 3, turn. **Next row** Sk first dc and ch-1, *V-st in next st, sk next dc and ch-1; rep from *, end sk last st, dc in 3rd ch of t-ch. Ch 3, turn. **Next row** Dc in first st, *sk next dc and ch-1, V-st in next st; rep from *, end, dc in 3rd ch of t-ch. Fasten off.

Left shoulder

Next row Sk 19 center V-sts, sk next dc and ch-1 of next V-St, join yarn with a sl st in next st, ch 3, dc in same st as joining, *sk next dc and ch-1, V-st in next st; rep from *, end sk last st, dc in 3rd ch of t-ch. Ch 3, turn. **Next row** Dc in first st, *sk next dc and ch-1, V-st in next st; rep from *, end sk next st, dc in 3rd ch of t-ch. Ch 3, turn. **Next row** Dc in first st, *sk next dc and ch-1, V-st in next st; rep from *, end sk last st, dc in 3rd ch of t-ch. Ch 3, turn. Fasten off.

FRONT

Work same as back until piece measures approx 21½ (22, 22½, 23)"/54.5 (56, 57, 58.5)cm from beg. Ch 3, turn.

Neck shaping

Left side

Next row Work in pat st across first 12 (14, 16, 20) V-sts, dc in next st. Ch 3, turn. **Next row** Sk first 2 dc and ch-1, *V-st in next st, sk next dc and ch-1; rep from *, end sk last st, dc in 3rd ch of t-ch. Ch 3, turn. **Next row** Work in pat st across first 11 (13, 15, 19) V-sts, dc in 3rd ch of t-ch . Ch 3, turn. **Next row** Sk first 2 dc and ch-1, *V-st in next st, sk next dc and ch-1; rep from *, end sk last st, dc in 3rd ch of t-ch. Ch 3, turn. Rep last 2 rows, working one less V-st every other row, until 8 (10, 12, 14) V-sts rem. Work even until piece measures same length as back to shoulder. Fasten off.

Right side

Next row Join yarn with a sl st in 3rd ch of ch-3 t-ch at side edge. Ch 3, dc in next st, cont to work in pat st across first 12 (14, 16, 20) V-sts, dc in next st. Ch 3, turn. Cont to work as for left side, reversing shaping.

SLEEVES

With larger hook, ch 58 (58, 64, 64). Row 1 Sc in 2nd ch from hook and in each ch across—57 (57, 63, 63) sts. Ch 1, turn. **Rows 2 and 4** Sc in each st across. Ch 3, turn. **Rows 3 and 5** Dc in each st across. Ch 1, turn. **Row 6** Sc in each st across. Ch 3, turn. Work row 1 of pat st—18 (18, 20, 20) V-sts. Beg with row 2, cont in pat st and

(Continued on page 134)

Simple, yet striking, Tricia McKenzie's cropped V-neck cardigan features an allover lace pattern and V-stitch edging. Slip it over a basic black dress for P.M. panache. "Short Take" first appeared in the Spring/Summer '02 issue of *Family Circle Easy Knitting* magazine.

MATERIALS

- *Lustersheen* by J&P Coats®, each approx 300yd/276m balls (cotton)
  4 (5) balls #1 white
- Size D/3 (3mm) crochet hook OR SIZE TO OBTAIN GAUGE
- Five ¹⁄₂"/13mm buttons

SIZES

Sized for Small/Medium (Large/X-Large).
Shown in size Small/Medium.

FINISHED MEASUREMENTS

- Bust (buttoned) 35¹⁄₂ (44)"/90 (112)cm
- Length 18¹⁄₂ (20)"/47 (51)cm
- Upper arm 16¹⁄₂ (18)"/42 (46)cm

GAUGE

2 lace pat reps to 4¹⁄₂"/11.5cm and 21 rows to 8"/20.5cm in lace pat using size D/3 (3mm) hook.
TAKE TIME TO CHECK YOUR GAUGE.

LACE PATTERN STITCH

Chain a multiple of 12 plus 6.
Row 1 (RS) (Dc, ch 2, dc) in 5th ch from hook, ch 4, skip next 5 ch,*(dc, ch 2, dc) in next ch for v-st, ch 4, skip next 5 ch; rep from * to last 2 ch, v-st in next ch, dc in last ch, turn. **Row 2** Ch 3, *work v-st in ch-2 sp of next v-st, ch 3, (3 dc, ch 2, 3 dc) in ch-2 sp of next v-st for shell, ch 3; rep from * to last v-st, v-st in ch-2 sp of last v-st, dc in top of t-ch, turn. **Row 3** Ch 3, *v-st in ch-2 sp of next v-st, ch 4, v-st in ch-2 sp of next shell, ch 4; rep from * to last v-st, v-st in ch-2 sp of last v-st, dc in top of t-ch, turn. Rep rows 2 and 3 for lace pat st.

BACK

Ch 102 (126). Work in lace pat on 8 (10) lace pat reps for 25 (27) rows. Cut yarn. Turn work.
Armhole shaping
With WS of work facing, rejoin yarn in first dc of 3rd v-st from beg of row, ch 3, [work v-st in next v-st, ch 3, work shell in next v-st, ch 3] 6 (8) times, work v-st in next v-st, dc in next ch, turn. Cont in lace pat st on these 6 (8) lace pats for 21 (23) rows more. Fasten off.

LEFT FRONT

Ch 54 (66). Work in lace pat on 4 (5) lace pat reps for 25 (27) rows.
Armhole and neck shaping
Row 1 (WS) Pat to last 3 v-sts, v-st in next v-st, dc in next ch, turn. **Row 2** Pat to last v-st, dc in last v-st, turn. **Row 3** Ch 6, work shell in next v-st, pat to end, turn. **Row 4** Pat to last shell, v-st in last shell, ch 2, dc in 3rd ch of t-ch, turn. **Row 5** Ch 3, work shell in next v-st, pat to end, turn. **Row 6** Pat to last shell, v-st in last shell, skip 2 dc, dc in next dc, turn. **Row 7** Ch 3, 3 dc in first v-st, pat to end, turn. **Row 8** Pat to last v-st, v-st in last v-st, ch 4, dc in top of t-ch, turn. **Row 9** Ch 6, v-st in next v-st, pat to end, turn. **Row 10** Pat to last v-st in last v-st, ch 2, dc in 3rd ch of t-ch, turn. **Row 11** Ch 3, v-st in first v-st, pat to end, turn. **Rows 12-15** Rep rows 2-5. **Row 16** Pat to last shell, v-st in last shell, ch 1, dc in top

of t-ch, turn. **Row 17** Ch 3, work shell in first v-st, pat to end, turn. Rep last 2 rows 2 (3) times more, then rep row 16 again. Fasten off.

RIGHT FRONT

Work as for left front (lace pat is reversible).

SLEEVES

Ch 54 (66). Work in lace pat on 4 (5) lace pats for 2 rows.
Sleeve shaping
Row 1 Ch 5, v-st in first v-st, pat to last v-st, v-st in last v-st, ch 2, dc in top of t-ch, turn. **Row 2** Ch 5, v-st in next v-st, pat to last v-st, v-st in last v-st, ch 2, dc in 3rd ch of t-ch, turn. **Rows 3 and 4** Rep row 2. **Row 5** Ch 7, v-st in next v-st, pat to last v-st, v-st in last v-st, ch 4, dc in 3rd ch of t-ch, turn. **Row 6** Ch 3, 2 dc in first dc, ch 3, v-st in next v-st pat to last v-st, v-st in last v-st, ch 3, 3 dc in 5th ch of t-ch, turn. **Row 7** Ch 5, dc in first dc, ch 4, v-st in next v-st, pat to last v-st, v-st in last v-st, ch 4, (dc, ch 2, dc) in top of t-ch, turn. **Row 8** Ch 5, 3 dc in first ch-2 sp, ch 3, v-st in next v-st, pat to last complete v-st, v-st in this v-st, ch 3, 3 dc in t-ch sp, ch 2, dc in 3rd ch of t-ch, turn. **Row 9** Ch 5, dc in first ch-2 sp, ch 4, v-st in next v-st, pat to last v-st, v-st in last v-st, ch 4, dc in t-ch sp, ch 2, dc in 3rd ch of t-ch, turn. **Row 10** Rep row 8. **Row 11** Ch 3, v-st in first ch-2 sp, pat to last v-st, v-st in last v-st, ch 4, v-st in

(Continued on page 132)

Soft Focus

for intermediate crocheters

Teamed with a bikini top, a flower-patterned skirt with scalloped edges and snap closures in back, makes a bold statement off the shoreline. Gradating hook sizes create the skimmy A-line shape. Designed by Mari Lynn Patrick, "Soft Focus" first appeared in the Spring/Summer '03 issue of *Family Circle Easy Knitting* magazine.

MATERIALS

- *Grandma's Best* by Caron International, 1.8oz/51g balls, each approx 350yd/323m (cotton) 4 (6, 6) balls in #157 cream
- One each sizes B/1, C/2, D/3 and E/4 (2, 2.5, 3 and 3.5mm) crochet hooks OR SIZE TO OBTAIN GAUGES
- 5 large plastic snap fasteners

SIZES

Sized for Small (Medium, Large). Shown in size Small.

FINISHED MEASUREMENTS

- Lower edge 45 (47, 50)"/114 (119, 127)cm
- Hip 36 (38, 40)"/91.5 (96.5, 101.5)cm
- Waist 29 (31, 32)"/73.5 (78.5, 81)cm
- Length (including edge) 22"/56cm

GAUGES

- 5 pat reps and 11 rows to 4"/10cm over flower pat st using 2 strands of yarn and size E/4 (3.5mm) crochet hook.
- 4 pat reps and 12 rows to 4"/10cm over flower pat st using 2 strands of yarn and size D/3 (3mm) crochet hook.

TAKE TIME TO CHECK YOUR GAUGES.

Note

Work with 2 strands of yarn held tog throughout.

FLOWER PATTERN STITCH

Ch a multiple of 8 sts plus 4.

Row 1 (RS) Work 1 sc in 2nd ch from hook, 1 sc in next ch, ch 9, 1 sc in next ch, ch 5, skip 5 ch, 1 sc in next ch, *[ch 9, 1 sc in next ch] twice, ch 5, skip next 5 ch, 1 sc in next ch; rep from * to last 2 ch, ch 9, 1 sc in each of last 2 ch, turn.

Row 2 Ch 7 (counts as 1 tr and ch 3), *1 sc in next ch-9 loop, ch 1, 1 sc in next ch-9 lp, ch 5; rep from *, end by working ch 3 instead of ch 5 at end of last rep, 1 tr in last sc, turn.

Row 3 Ch 1, 1 sc in first tr, ch 3, * 1 sc in next sc, ch 9, 1 sc in next ch-1 sp, ch 9, 1 sc in next sc, ch 5; rep from *, end by working ch 3 instead of ch 5 at end of last rep, 1 sc in 4th ch of ch-1 at beg of previous row, turn.

Row 4 Ch 5 (counts as 1 tr and ch 1), *1 sc in next ch-9 lp, ch 5, 1 sc in next ch-9 lp, ch 1; rep from *, end 1 tr in last sc, turn.

Row 5 Ch 1, 1 sc in first tr, 1 sc in next ch-1 sp, ch 9, 1 sc in next sc, ch 5, *1 sc in next sc, ch 9, 1 sc in next ch-1 sp, ch 9, 1 sc in next sc, ch 5; rep from * to last sc, 1 sc in last sc, ch 9, 1 sc in last ch sp, 1 sc in 4th ch of ch-5 at beg of previous row.

Rep rows 2-5 for flower pat st.

BACK

With size E/4 (3.5mm) hook, and 2 strands of yarn, ch 148 (156, 164). Work in flower pat st on 18 (19, 20) pats for 23 rows (8"/20.5cm). Change to size D/3 (3mm) hook and work in pat st for 7"/18cm more, ending with pat row 2 or 4. Change to size C/2 (2.5mm) hook and work in pat st for 3"/7.5cm more, end with pat row 5. Dec for top of skirt in progressive pat rows as foll: **Dec (pat row 2)** Ch 6 (counts as 1 dc and ch 3), *1 sc in next ch-9 lp, ch 1, 1 sc in next ch-9 lp, ch 4; rep from *, end by working ch 2 instead of ch 4 at end of last rep, 1 dc in last sc, turn. **Dec (pat row 3)** Ch 1, 1 sc in first dc, ch 2, *1 sc in next sc, ch 9, 1 sc in next ch-1 sp, ch 9, 1 sc in next sc, ch 4; rep from *, end by working ch 2 instead of ch 4 at end of last rep, 1 sc in 3rd ch of ch-6 at beg of previous row. **Dec (pat row 4)** Ch 4 (counts as 1 dc and ch 1), *1 sc in next ch-9 lp, ch 4, 1 sc in next ch-9 lp, ch 1; rep from *, end 1 dc in last sc, turn. **Dec (pat row 5)** Ch 1, 1 sc in first dc, 1 sc in next ch-1 sp, ch 9, 1 sc in next sc, ch 4, * 1 sc in next sc, ch 9, 1 sc in next ch-1 sp, ch 9, 1 sc in next sc, ch 4; rep from * to last sc, 1 sc in last sc, ch 9, 1 sc in last ch sp, 1 sc in 3rd ch of ch-4 at beg of previous row. **Dec (pat row 2)** Ch 5 (counts as 1 dc and ch 2), *1 sc in next ch-9 lp, ch 1, 1 sc in next ch-9 lp, ch 3; rep from *, end by working ch 1 instead of ch 3 at end of last rep, 1 dc in last sc. Fasten off.

FRONT

Work as for back.

FINISHING

Working from WS with size D/3 (3mm) crochet hook, sl st the right side seam of skirt tog. Fasten off.

Placket and waistband

Beg at 7"/18cm from the waist of front side seam, with 2 strands of yarn and size D/3 (3mm) hook, work front placket inserting hook approx 1/2"/1.25cm from seam edge, work 30 sc along this edge (for a 1/2"/1.25cm wide front placket), then work 3 sc in top corner, hdc evenly across waistband of front and back. Cut

(Continued on page 135)

Vest Dressed

for intermediate crocheters

Bound for the beach or out about town, Helene Rush's lace-patterned V-neck vest is the ideal layering piece. With a simple box shape and a relaxed silhouette, it provides comfort plus style in one pretty package. "Vest Dressed" first appeared in the Spring/Summer '98 issue of *Family Circle Easy Knitting* magazine.

MATERIALS

- *Beehive Baby* by Patons®, 1³/₄oz/50g balls, each approx 304yd/278m (acrylic)
  4 (4, 5) balls in #3430 white
- Size D/3 (3mm) crochet hook
- Six ⁵/₈"/16mm buttons

SIZES

Sized for Small (Medium, Large). Shown in size Medium.

FINISHED MEASUREMENTS

- Bust 33¹/₂ (38¹/₂, 43)"/85 (98, 109)cm
- Length 18¹/₂ (19, 19¹/₂)"/47 (48.5, 49.5)cm

GAUGE

5 lace pats and 19 rows to 6"/15.25cm over lace pat st using size D/3 (3mm) hook. TAKE TIME TO CHECK YOUR GAUGE.

STITCHES USED

Lace Pattern Stitch

(Chain a multiple of 10 plus 4)

Row 1 Dc in 4th ch from hook, *ch 3, skip next 4 ch, (sc, ch 3, 3 dc) in next ch for square, skip next 4 ch, (dc, ch 1, dc) in next ch for v-st; rep from *, end last rep by 2 dc (instead of v-st) in last ch, turn. **Row 2** Ch 3, dc in first dc, *ch 3, skip next 3-dc square, work square in ch-3 sp of square, skip next ch-3 sp, work v-st in ch-1 sp of next v-st; rep from *, end last rep by 2 dc in top of t-ch. Rep row 2 for lace pat st.

BACK

Ch 144 (164, 184). Work in lace pat on 14 (16, 18) lace pats until piece measures 11"/28cm from beg.

Armhole shaping

Row 1 Ch 1, sl st across to ch-1 sp of first v-st, work from * on row 2 of lace pat st to last v-st, work 1 dc in ch-1 sp of v-st, leave rem sts unworked, turn. **Row 2** Work from * on row 2 of lace pat st to last square, do not ch 3, work sc in ch-3 sp of square, turn. **Row 3** Ch 3, v-st in next v-st, work in pat to last square, do not ch 3, dc in ch-3 sp of square, turn. **Row 4** (Sl st, ch 3, dc) in ch-1 sp of first v-st, work in pat across, ending with 2 dc in last v-st, turn. Cont in lace pat st on 10 (12, 14) lace pats until armhole measures 7¹/₂ (8, 8¹/₂)"/19 (20.5, 21.5)cm. **Finishing row** Ch 3, dc in first dc, *ch 3, sc in ch-3 sp of next square, ch 3, v-st in ch-1 sp of next v-st; rep from * end with 2 dc in top of t-ch. Fasten off.

LEFT FRONT

Ch 74 (84, 94). Work in lace pat on 7 (8, 9) lace pats until piece measures 11"/28cm from beg.

Armhole and neck shaping

Row 1 Ch 3, square in ch-3 sp of next square, work in pat to last v-st, dc in ch-1 sp of v-st, turn, leaving rem sts unworked for armhole. **Row 2** Ch 3, square in ch-3 sp of next square, work in pat to last square, do not ch 3, dc in ch-3 sp of square, turn. **Row 3** Ch 3, v-st in ch-1 sp of v-st, work in pat to last square, do not ch 3, dc in ch-3 sp of square, turn. **Row 4** Ch 3, v-st in ch-1 sp of v-st, work in pat to last v-st, dc in ch-1 sp of v-st, turn. **Row 5** Ch 3, square in ch-3 sp of next square, work to last v-st, 2 dc in ch-1 sp of v-st, turn. **Row 6** Work in pat to last square, do not ch 3, dc in ch-3 sp of square, turn. **Row 7** Ch 3, v-st in ch-1 sp of v-st, work in pat to end of row, turn. **Row 8** Work in pat to last v-st, dc in ch-1 sp of v-st, turn. **Row 9** Ch 3, square in ch-3 sp of next square, work in pat to end of row, turn. **Rows 10 and 11** Rep rows 6 and 7. **Row 12** Work in pat, beg and ending in center of first and last v-st—2 (3, 4) lace pats. Cont until same length as Back to shoulder, ending with Finishing row.

RIGHT FRONT

Work as for left front (pat is reversible).

FINISHING

Steam pieces very lightly. Sew shoulder and side seams.

Armhole bands

Join at underarm, ch 1 and sc evenly around armhole, join with sl st to first sc. **Rnd 2** Ch 1, sc in each sc around, join. **Rnd 3** Ch 3, dc in each sc around, join with sl st to top of ch-3. **Rnd 4** Rep rnd 2. **Rnd 5** Ch 5, working from left to right, work reverse sc as foll: *work sc in next sc, ch 1, skip 1 sc; rep from * around. Join and fasten off.

(Continued on page 132)

Bare Essential

for intermediate crocheters

Dressed up or down, an airy crochet top in a muted desert-hue delivers a flirty touch. Designed by Sandy Prosser, the flower motifs are joined together with slip stitches. Shell-stitch edging is a fetching finale. "Bare Essential" first appeared in the Spring/Summer '03 issue of *Family Circle Easy Knitting* magazine.

MATERIALS

- *Cable 2005* by Sesia/LBUSA, 3³/₄oz/50g balls, each approx 146yd/135m (cotton)
  4 (5, 6) balls in #78 peach
- Size B/1 (2mm) crochet hook OR SIZE TO OBTAIN GAUGE

SIZES

Sized for Small (Medium, Large). Shown in size Small.

FINISHED MEASUREMENTS

- Bust 28 (31½, 35)"/71 (80, 89)cm
- Length 18 (20¼, 22½)"/45.5 (51.5, 57)cm

GAUGES

Small

- One motif to 2"/5cm using size B/1 (2mm) crochet hook.

Medium

- One motif to 2¼"/5.7cm using size B/1 (2mm) crochet hook.

Large

- One motif to 2½"/6.4cm using size B/1 (2mm) crochet hook.

TAKE TIME TO CHECK YOUR GAUGE.

SMALL TOP

Half motif

(make 4)

Ch 5 (counts as first tr and one foundation ch). **Row 1 (WS)** Work 10 tr in 4th ch (foundation ch) from hook. Ch 15 (counts as 1 tr and ch 11), turn. **Row 2** Sk first st, [2 tr in next st, tr in next st, ch 5, 2 tr in next st, tr in next st, ch 11] twice, end tr in last st. Fasten off. Set aside.

Motif A

(make 1)

Ch 5 (counts as first tr and one foundation ch). **Rnd 1 (RS)** Work 16 tr in 4th ch (foundation ch)

from hook. Join rnd with a sl st in 4th ch of first tr. **Rnd 2** Ch 4 (counts as 1 tr), tr in same ch as sl st, [tr in next st, ch 11, 2 tr in next st, tr in next st, ch 5, 2 tr in next st] 3 times, end tr in next st, ch 11, 2 tr in next st, tr in next st, ch 5. Join rnd with a sl st in 4th ch of ch-4. Fasten off.

Motif B

(make 101)

Work as for motif A to rnd 2. **Rnd 2 (joining)** Ch 4 (counts as 1 tr), tr in same ch as sl st, tr in next st, ch 5, sl st in ch-11 lp of motif A, ch 5, 2 tr in next st, tr in next st, ch 2, sl in ch-5 lp of motif A, ch 2, 2 tr in next st, ch 5, sl in ch-11 lp of motif A, ch 5, [2 tr in next st, tr in next st, ch 5, 2 tr in next st, tr in next st, ch 11] twice, end 2 tr in next st, tr in next st, ch 5. Join rnd with a sl st in 4th ch of ch-4. Fasten off. Cont to join motifs following placement diagram. At adjacent ch-11 lps, join motifs with ch 5, sl st in ch-11, ch 5. To prevent bulk at ch-11 joinings, sl st into the previous sl st. At adjacent ch-5 lps, join motifs with ch 2, sl st in ch-5, ch 2. Join half motifs at front neck edge in the same manner.

MEDIUM TOP

Half motif

(make 4)

Ch 6 (counts as first dtr and one foundation ch). **Row 1 (WS)** Work 10 dtr in 5th ch (foundation ch) from hook. Ch 16 (counts as 1 dtr and ch 11), turn. **Row 2** Sk first st, [2 dtr in next st, dtr in next st, ch 5, 2 dtr in next st, dtr in next st,

ch 11] twice, end dtr in last st. Fasten off. Set aside.

Motif A

(make 1)

Ch 6 (counts as first dtr and one foundation ch). **Rnd 1 (RS)** Work 16 dtr in 5th ch (foundation ch) from hook. Join rnd with a sl st in 5th ch of first dtr. **Rnd 2** Ch 5 (counts as 1 dtr), dtr in same ch as sl st, [dtr in next st, ch 11, 2 dtr in next st, dtr in next st, ch 5, 2 dtr in next st] 3 times, end dtr in next st, ch 11, 2 dtr in next st, dtr in next st, ch 5. Join rnd with a sl st in 5th ch of ch-5. Fasten off.

Motif B

(make 101)

Work as for motif A to rnd 2. **Rnd 2 (joining)** Ch 5 (counts as 1 dtr), dtr in same ch as sl st, dtr in next st, ch 5, sl st in ch-11 lp of motif A, ch 5, 2 dtr in next st, dtr in next st, ch 2, sl in ch-5 lp of motif A, ch 2, 2 dtr in next st, ch 5, sl in ch-11 lp of motif A, ch 5, [2 dtr in next st, dtr in next st, ch 5, 2 dtr in next st, dtr in next st, ch 11] twice, end 2 dtr in next st, dtr in next st, ch 5. Join rnd with a sl st in 5th ch of ch-5. Fasten off. Cont to join motifs following placement diagram. At adjacent ch-11 lps, join motifs with ch 5, sl st in ch-11, ch 5. To prevent bulk at ch-11 joinings, sl st into the previous sl st. At adjacent ch-5 lps, join motifs with ch 2, sl st in ch-5, ch 2. Join half motifs at front neck edge in the same manner.

(Continued on page 135)

Extra Credit

Whip up fun, fast and fabulous accessories.

Shore Thing
for intermediate crocheters

Mary Jane Protus's playful tote is perfect for a day filled with sand and sun. It's made up of lacy medallions bordered by a reverse single crochet stitch; rustic wooden beads trim the drawstring tie. "Shore Thing" first appeared in the Spring/Summer '00 issue of *Family Circle Easy Knitting* magazine.

MATERIALS
- *Cotton Connection D.K. No.2* by Naturally/S.R. Kertzer, Ltd., 1¾oz/50g balls, each approx 108yd/100m (cotton/wool/nylon)
  3 balls in #02 natural
- One each sizes G/6 and H/8 (4.5mm and 5mm) crochet hooks OR SIZE TO OBTAIN GAUGE
- 2 wood beads

FINISHED MEASUREMENTS
- 9"/23cm square

GAUGE
1 square to 3"/7.5cm using smaller crochet hook.
TAKE TIME TO CHECK YOUR GAUGE.

Note
Squares are joined as they are worked. Work as indicated on diagram foll squares 1-9 for back, then rep for front.

BAG
(make 2 pieces)
First square (A)
With smaller crochet hook, ch 8, join with sl st to form ring. **Rnd 1 Ch 3, 19 dc into ring, join with sl st to 3rd ch of beg ch. **Rnd 2** Ch 4, [dc 1 into next dc, ch 1] 19 times, end rnd with sl st into 3rd ch.** **Rnd 3** Sl st into next ch-1 space, ch 10, skip next ch-1 space (1 dc, 1 ch and 1 dc from previous rnd), *[2 dc into next ch-1 space] 4 times, ch 7 (corner), skip next ch-1 space, rep from * twice more; [2 dc into next ch-1 space] 3 times, 1 dc into next ch-1 space, sl st in 3rd ch. Fasten off.

Join one side square (B)
Work as for first square from ** to **. **Rnd 3** Sl st into next ch-1 space, ch 10, skip next ch-1 space (1 dc, 1 ch and 1 dc from previous rnd), [2 dc into next ch-1 space] 4 times, ch 3, holding square to the right (or above) of square being joined, sl st

into 4th ch of square being joined, ch 3, skip next ch-1 space, [2 dc into next ch-1 space] 2 times; join by sl st into space between 4th and 5th dc of square being joined; [2 dc into next ch-1 space] 2 times; ch 3, sl st into 4th ch of square being joined, ch 3, skip next ch-1 space, [2 dc into next ch-1 space] 4 times, ch 7, [2 dc into next ch-1 space] 3 times, 1 dc into next ch-1 space, sl st in 3rd ch. Fasten off.

Join 2 sides square (C)
Work as for first square from ** to **. **Rnd 3** Sl st into next ch-1 space, ch 10, skip next ch-1 space (1 dc, 1 ch and 1 dc from previous rnd), [2 dc into next ch-1 space] 4 times, *ch 3, holding square to the right (or above) of square being joined, sl st into 4th ch of square being joined, ch 3, skip next ch-1 space, [2 dc into next ch-1 space] 2 times; join by sl st into space between 4th and 5th dc of square being joined; [2 dc into next ch-1 space] 2 times*; rep from * once more; ch 3, sl st into 4th ch of square being joined, ch 3, skip next ch-1 space, [2dc into next ch-1 space] 3 times, 1 dc into next ch-1 space, sl st in 3rd ch. Fasten off.

FINISHING
With WS tog, 2 strands of yarn and larger crochet hook, join sides and bottom edge by working 1 row reverse sc. Fasten off.
With RS of bag facing, 2 strands of yarn and larger crochet hook, work 1 rnd reverse sc around upper edge, beg at side seam. Fasten off.

STRAPS
With smaller crochet hook and 1 strand of yarn, join yarn with sl st to top edge of bag at side seam, ch 75, join with 1 sc at opposite side seam. Make 3 more straps, always join with sc at side seams. Fasten off.

Slide for straps
With smaller crochet hook and 1 strand of yarn, ch 12, turn, 1 dc in 4th ch from hook, work 1 dc into each ch to end. Fasten off, leaving longer tail for seam. Wrap slide around all straps, sew seam.

Drawstring
With smaller crochet hook and 1 strand of yarn, ch 175. Fasten off.
Thread in and out at top edge, beg at center front. Slip 1 bead onto each end, secure with knot.

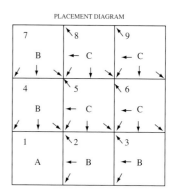

PLACEMENT DIAGRAM

Shawl Savvy

for beginner crocheters

Gorgeous hand-dyed chenille makes the most of Mari Lynn Patrick's quick-crocheting shawl design. Worked in multiple strands using an oversized crochet hook, it's a chic cover-up for a nippy summer eve. "Shawl Savvy" first appeared in the Spring/Summer '99 issue of *Family Circle Easy Knitting* magazine.

MATERIALS

- *Isis* by Colinette/Unique Kolours, 3½oz/100g skeins, each approx 108yd/100m (viscose) 5 skeins in #83 lilac
- Size K/10½ (7mm) crochet hook OR SIZE TO OBTAIN GAUGE

FINISHED MEASUREMENTS

- 18½" wide x 70" long/47cm x 178cm

GAUGE

7 pat spaces and 22 rows to 10"/25.5cm over pat st using size K/10½ (7mm) hook.
TAKE TIME TO CHECK YOUR GAUGE

Note

Shawl will stretch lengthwise after wearing.

SHAWL

Beg at one short end, ch 55 loosely. **Row 1** Work 1 sc in 7th ch from hook, *ch 3, skip 3 ch, sc in next ch (for 1 pat space); rep from * 11 times more—13 pat spaces (including turning ch-7 at beg of row). Ch 4, turn. **Row 2** Work 1 sc in first sc, *ch 3, work 1 sc in next sc; rep from *, ending with 1 sc in 4th ch of ch-7. Ch 4, turn. **Row 3** Work 1 sc in first sc, *ch 3, work 1 sc in next sc; rep from * to last space, work 1 sc in 4th ch of ch-4. Ch 4, turn. Rep this row for pat st until piece measures 70"/178cm from beg. Fasten off.

FINISHING

Do not steam block. Lay flat to measurements, mist lightly and allow to dry.

Back Splash

for intermediate crocheters

Step out in style with Kellie Overby's soft take on the backpack. Done up in an easy-to-crochet shell-pattern and finished with mesh straps and beaded chain-stitch ties, it's a real attention-getter. "Back Splash" first appeared in the Spring/Summer '00 issue of *Family Circle Easy Knitting* magazine.

MATERIALS

- *Cotton Connection D.K. No.3* by Naturally/S.R. Kertzer, Ltd., $1^3/_4$oz/50g balls, each approx 120yd/111m (cotton/linen)
  4 balls in #03 natural
- Size E/4 (3.5mm) crochet hook OR SIZE TO OBTAIN GAUGE
- 4 wood beads 16mm

FINISHED MEASUREMENTS

$10^1/_2$"/26.5cm square (closed)

GAUGE

$3^1/_2$ reps and $13^1/_2$ rows to 4"/10cm over main pat using size E/4 (3.5mm) crochet hook. TAKE TIME TO CHECK YOUR GAUGE.

BACKPACK

FRONT

Ch 61 for base.
Beg main pat
Row 1 (RS) Skip 3 ch, 2 dc in next ch, skip 2 ch, 1 sc in next ch, *skip 2 ch, 4 dc in next ch, skip 2 ch, 1 sc in next ch; rep from * to end, turn.
Row 2 Ch 3, 2 dc in last sc, *1 sc between 2nd and 3rd dc of next 4-dc group, 4 dc in next sc; rep from * across, 1 sc in 3rd ch from previous row, turn. Rep row 2 until piece measures $10^1/_2$"/26.5cm from beg (36 rows have been worked). Fasten off.

BACK

With RS facing, turn front upside down, cont working from base as foll: **Row 1 (RS)** Skip first 9 sc, join yarn, ch 3, 2 dc in join or first sc, skip 2 ch, 1 sc in next ch, *skip 2 ch, 4 dc in next ch, skip 2 ch, 1 sc in next ch; rep from * until 6 reps have been worked, turn. Rep row 2 of main pat until piece measures 2"/5cm from beg of back. Fasten off. Fold spare corners of bottom front inwards, sew spare 9 sc on either end of bottom front along 2"/5cm edges of back just worked. Work in main pat over entire width as for front until back measures same as front when folded in half at base. Place markers on both sides for beg of flap.

Flap

Cont in pat for 20 more rows. Fasten off.

FINISHING

Sew side seams.

STRAP

(make 2)
Ch 12. **Row 1 (RS)** Skip 2 ch, 1 sc into next ch, *ch 1, skip 1 ch, 1 sc into next ch; rep from * to end, turn. **Row 2** Ch 2, *1 sc into next ch from previous row, ch 1; rep from * across, 1 sc into next ch, turn. Rep row 2 until strap measures 17"/43cm, or desired length. Fasten off.
Sew on straps, one end of strap to top of backpack (at marker), the other end along shaped bottom corner.

Ties (make 4)

Ch for approx 10"/25.5cm. Fasten off. Sew one tie each to corners of flap. With flap closed place markers on each side of bag corresponding with flap ties. Sew on rem two ties. Sl one wood bead on to each tie, knot end.

Stripe it Up

for beginner crocheters

It takes just four skeins of yarn to stitch up Jacquelyn Smyth's cheery striped tote. Day-Glo acrylic handles add a fun, funky finish. "Stripe it Up" first appeared in the Spring/Summer '02 issue of *Family Circle Easy Knitting* magazine.

MATERIALS

- *Raffia* by Judi & Co., each approx 72yd/65m (rayon) 1 ball each in red, orange, pink and dk pink
- Size F/5 (3.75mm) crochet hook OR SIZE TO OBTAIN GAUGE
- One silver and 2 gold safety pins
- One pair 5½"/14cm horseshoe handles by Judi & Co.
- 20"/51cm-length of ⅝"/16mm-wide satin ribbon in fuchsia
- Red sewing thread
- 5"/12.5cm x 9"/23cm piece of matboard
- 6"/15cm x 10"/25.5cm piece of cotton fabric in red
- 5"/12.5cm x 9"/23cm piece of fusible web
- Double-sided carpet tape

FINISHED MEASUREMENTS

- Approx 8½"/21.5cm tall (not including handles) and 11"/28cm across top edge

GAUGE

16 sts and 17 rows to 4"/10cm over sc using size F/5 (3.75mm) crochet hook.
TAKE TIME TO CHECK YOUR GAUGE.

Notes

1 For ease in working, wind skeins of raffia into balls. Place each ball in a quart-size, zipper-lock plastic storage bag. Zip bag closed, leaving a small opening. Pull raffia strand through opening in bag.
2 When changing colors, draw new color though 2 lps on hook to complete sc.

TOTE BAG

Beg at center bottom, with A, ch 20. **Rnd 1** Sc in 2nd ch from hook and in next 17 ch, work 3 sc in last ch; mark 2nd of these last 3 sts with a gold safety pin for corner st. Turn to bottom of ch. Working through bottom lps of ch, sc in next 18 lps, work 3 sc in last lp; mark 2nd of these last 3 sts with a gold safety pin for corner st—42 sts. Mark last st made with silver safety pin to indicate end of rnd. **Rnd 2** Sc in each st around, working 3 sc in each corner st and marking 2nd of these 3 sts with safety pin—46 sts. **Rnds 3-8** Rep rnd 2, joining B when rnd 8 is completed—70 sts. **Rnds 9 and 10** With B, [sc in each st to within 2 sts of corner st, work 2 sc in next st, sc in next 3 sts, marking 2nd of these 3 sts with safety pin, work 2 sc in next st] twice, sc in each st to end of rnd—78 sts. **Rnd 11** Rep rnd 9, removing corner safety pins—82 sts. Trace outline of bottom of bag onto matboard for bottom liner; set aside. **Rnds 12 and 13** Sc in each st around, joining C when rnd 13 is completed.

Stripe pattern

Working even around, work as foll: 3 rnds C, 1 rnd A, 3 rnds D, 1 rnd A, 3 rnds B and 1 rnd A. Rep these 12 rnds once more, then work 3 rnds C, 1 rnd A, 3 rnds D and 1 rnd A. Join last rnd with a sl st in next st. Fasten off.

FINISHING

Draw in all loose ends. Cut ribbon into 4 equal lengths for tabs. For each handle, thread tab through holes; even up raw ends and pin to secure. On WS, pin tabs to top edge of bag, so bottom edge of handle is ½"/1.5cm from top edge of bag and handle is centered from side to side. Using thread doubled in sewing needle, sew each tab to bag along last rnd using backstitches. Fold raw ends of each tab to WS, then over-cast st in place along side and bottom edges.

Bottom liner

Following tracing of bottom of bag, cut out matboard shape for liner. Fuse web to center of WS of fabric. Trace liner onto center of fused side of fabric. Cut out shape ½"/1.5cm larger all around. Fuse fabric to liner. Clip fabric at ½"/1.5cm intervals all around. Fold fabric to WS of liner and fuse in place. Adhere strips of carpet tape to WS of liner. Insert liner into bottom of bag.

Summer Shoppers

for intermediate crocheters

Maria Matteucci's colorful crochet duo has summer in the bag. The square tote sports a tasseled handle and a medley of stitches; the airy knapsack secures with a snap closure and a corded drawstring with an adjustable stay. "Summer Shoppers" first appeared in the Spring/Summer '98 issue of *Family Circle Easy Knitting* magazine.

MATERIALS

- *Berella "4"* by Spinrite, 3½oz/100g balls, each approx 240yd/219m (acrylic)

Square Tote

- 3 balls in #8821 green
- Size F/5 (4mm) crochet hook OR SIZE TO OBTAIN GAUGE
- 1yd/1m of matching lining fabric
- 2yd ½"/1.25cm horsehair braid
- Large snap closure
- One 11¼" x 3¾"/28.5 x 9.5cm plastic or heavy cardboard for base insert

Knapsack

- 4 balls in #8853 lilac
- One each sizes B/1 and F/5 (2 and 4mm) crochet hooks OR SIZE TO OBTAIN GAUGE
- 1yd/1m of matching lining fabric
- Large snap closure
- 2 small buttons

FINISHED MEASUREMENTS

Square Tote

- 10" long x 12" wide/25.5cm x 30.5cm
- Gusset measures 4"/10cm wide.

Knapsack

- Bottom diameter 12"/30.5cm
- Depth 12"/30.5cm

GAUGE

Square Tote

18 dc to 4"/10cm and 17 dc rows to 8"/20cm over dc pat using size F/5 (4mm) hook.

Knapsack

18 dc to 4"/10cm and 10 dc rnds to 4½"/11.5cm using larger hook.

TAKE TIME TO CHECK YOUR GAUGE.

SQUARE TOTE

GUSSETS AND BOTTOM

Ch 20. **Row 1** Dc in 4th ch from hook and in each ch to end—18 dc, counting t-ch as 1 dc. Ch 3, turn. **Row 2** Skip first dc, 1 dc in each dc, end 1 dc in top of t-ch. Ch 3, turn. Rep row 2 until there are 67 rows from beg. Fasten off.

FRONT

Place 4 markers on each side of row 22 and row 46 of gusset piece to mark center 25 rows of piece (this marks bottom of bag). Working across one side from marker to marker, work 51 sc evenly along one side of bottom. Ch 3, turn. Work even in 51 dc for 7 rows more. **Row 9** Ch 4, skip first 2 dc, *dc in next dc, ch 1, skip next dc; rep from *, end dc in top of t-ch—25 mesh sps. **Rows 10 and 11** Ch 4, *dc in next dc, ch 1; rep from *end dc in top of t-ch. **Row 12** Ch 4, skip first dc mesh sp, dc in next dc, work dc mesh to last dc mesh sp, skip last dc mesh sp, turn. **Row 13** Rep row 12—21 mesh sps. **Rows 14 and 15** Work even in mesh pat. **Row 16** Ch 3, work 1 dc in each dc and in each ch-1 sp to end—43 dc. Work even in dc for 6 rows more. Fasten off.

BACK

Working along other side of bottom, between opposite markers, work as for front.

FINISHING

Pin to measurements and steam lightly. Working from RS over horsehair braid, sc one gusset to side of front, cont to sc across gusset (at bottom edge), sc other gusset to side of back. Repeat for other side of bag. Secure ends. Working from left to right, work reverse sc edge around top of bag.

Handles

(make 2)

Cut 4 lengths of yarn to form into a twisted cord 21"/53cm long. Form one end into a 1½"/4cm tassel. Knot and fringe opposite end to make a tassel to match. Make a chain the length of the twisted cord. Hold chain underneath twisted cord and working over cord and through 1 ch at same time, work 1 sc around cord and through each ch. Fasten off. Secure handles to bag for 2"/5cm at top, at center 5½"/14cm of bag. Cut fabric to cover base insert with ½"/1.25cm seam allowance and hand-sew to fit. Cut fabric to match front and back pieces and gusset and bottom piece with a seam allowance of ½"/1.25cm. Seam gusset to front and back pieces. Press lining down

(Continued on page 136)

Tote-a-Tote

for intermediate crocheters

This perky pair designed by Maria Matteucci is made for a life spent on the go. Choose from a fabric-lined patchwork of crochet posies or a structured sack with a button closure. Both are as pretty as they are practical. "Tote-a-Tote" first appeared in the Spring/Summer '98 issue of *Family Circle Easy Knitting* magazine.

MATERIALS

Patchwork Tote

- *Canadiana* by Patons®, 3¹/₂oz/100g balls, each approx 228yd/208m (acrylic)
  4 balls in #3570 turquoise
- Size E/4 (3.5mm) crochet hook OR SIZE TO OBTAIN GAUGE
- 1yd/1m of matching lining fabric
- Large snap closure

Sack

- *Wintuk* by Caron International, 3¹/₂oz/99g skeins, each approx 213yd/196m (acrylic)
  4 skeins in #3255 periwinkle blue
- Size E/4 (3.5mm) crochet hook OR SIZE TO OBTAIN GAUGE
- 1yd/1m of matching lining fabric
- One ⁷/₈"/22mm button
- 1yd/1m flexible plastic ¹/₄"/6mm tube

FINISHED MEASUREMENTS

Patchwork Tote

- 12¹/₂" long x 11" wide/32cm x 28cm

Sack

- Bottom piece 7" long x 4" wide/18cm x 10cm
- 11" tall x 15"wide at top/28cm x 38cm

GAUGES

Patchwork Tote

One square to 3¹/₂"/9cm square using size E/4 (3.5mm) hook.

Sack

15 sc and 21 rows to 4"/10cm over woven pat st using size E/4 (3.5mm) hook.

TAKE TIME TO CHECK YOUR GAUGE.

PATCHWORK TOTE

SQUARE

(Make 18)

Beg at center, ch 8, join with sl st to first ch to form ring. **Rnd 1** Working into ring, *work 1 sc into ring, ch 3; rep from * 7 times more, end sl st into top of sc—8 lps. **Rnd 2** Ch 4, holding lp from previous rnd forward and working into beg ring from behind, *work 1 sc in ring, ch 4; rep from * 6 times more, end sl st into ring—8 lps. **Rnd 3** In each ch-4 lp, work 1 sc, ch 1, 2 dc, ch 1, 1 sl st—8 petals. Join with sl st to first sc. **Rnd 4** *Ch 4, holding petal from previous rnd forward, work 1 sc around sc post from behind; rep from * 7 times more—8 lps. Join with sl st to first lp. **Rnd 5** Rep rnd 3. **Rnd 6** *Work 1 sc in first ch-1 sp of petal, ch 8, skip 2 dc, 1 sc in next ch-1 sp of same petal (corner), ch 4, 1 sc in between 2 dc of next petal, ch 4; rep from * 3 times more, join with sl st to first sc. **Rnd 7** *Work 4 sc, ch 1, 4 sc in ch-8 lp, [4 sc in ch-4 lp] twice; rep from *, join with sl st to first sc. **Rnd 8** Ch 1, work 1 sc in each sc and 3 sc in each ch-1 corner sp around. Fasten off.

FINISHING

Pin squares to measurements and steam lightly. Sew squares tog with 3 sets and rows of squares each for back and front. Sew front and back tog along 3 sides.

Top edge

Sc evenly around top edge of bag. Join with sl st, ch 1. Work 7 more rnds sc. Fasten off.

Straps

(make 2)

Ch 100. Sc in 2nd ch from hook and each ch to end. Do not turn, but working into other side (beg lps) of ch, work 1 sc in each lp to end, 2 sc in last lp. Then work 1 sc in each sc all around both sides (with 2 sc in other corner). Fasten off. Overlap each strap by 3"/7.5cm from top of bag centering each side of center square. Sew to bag. Cut lining fabric 24"/61cm long by 23"/59cm wide. Fold in half lengthwise and with ¹/₂"/1.25cm seams, sew along one long side and lower edge. Press 1"/2.5cm at top to WS. Hand-sew lining to inside of bag ¹/₂"/1.25cm down from top. Sew snap inside at center for closing.

SACK

BOTTOM PIECE

Ch 15. **Rnd 1** Work 2 sc in 2nd ch from hook, sc in each of next 12 ch, 2 sc in last ch, do not turn, but turn ch upside down and working

(Continued on page 136)

Wrap Star

for intermediate crocheters

From ship to shore, this timeless beauty is sure to make wares. Designed by Pat Harste, this vintage classic features a triple cross-stitch pattern trimmed with a sweet ruffled border. "Wrap Star" first appeared in the Spring/Summer '03 issue of *Family Circle Easy Knitting* magazine.

MATERIALS

- *Helen's* Lace by Lorna's Laces Yarns, 4oz/125g hanks, each approx 1250yd/1143m (silk/wool) 2 hanks #10 peach
- Size E/4 (3.5mm) crochet hook OR SIZE TO OBTAIN GAUGE

FINISHED MEASUREMENTS

66"/167.5cm wide by 38"/96.5cm long

GAUGE

30 sts and 13 rows to 4"/10cm over pat st using size E/4 (3.5mm) crochet hook.
TAKE TIME TO CHECK YOUR GAUGE.

STITCHES USED

TC triple cross

Sk next 2 sts. Dc in 3rd st, dc in 2nd st sk, dc in first st sk.

SHAWL

Beg at bottom point, ch 8.
Row 1(WS) Work 2 dc in 4th ch from hook, dc in next 3 ch, work 2 dc in last ch—7 sts. Ch 3, turn. **Row 2** Work 3 dc in first st, dc in next st, TC over next 3 sts, dc in next st, work 3 dc in last st—11 sts. Ch 3, turn. **Row 3** Work 3 dc in first st, *TC over next 3 sts; rep from *, end work 3 dc in last st—15 sts. Ch 3, turn. **Row 4** Work 3 dc in first st, dc in next 2 sts, *TC over next 3 sts; rep from *, end dc in next 2 sts, work 3 dc in last st—19 sts. Ch 3, turn. **Row 5** Work 3 dc in first st, dc in next st, *TC over next 3 sts; rep from *, end dc in next st, work 3 dc in last st—23 sts. Ch 3, turn. **Row 6** Work 3 dc in first st, *TC over next 3 sts; rep from *, end work 3 dc in last st— sts. Ch 3, turn. Rep rows 4-6 35 times more— 111 rows completed (piece should measure approx 35"/89cm from beg).

Edging

Ch 1, turn. **Rnd 1(RS)** Sc in each dc across last row made, then making sure that work lies flat, sc evenly across each side edge. Join rnd with a sl st in ch-1. Ch 5, turn. Work back and forth across side edges only.

Ruffle

Row 1 (WS) Sk first st, sc in next st, *ch 5, sk next st, sc in next st; rep from * to end. Ch 5, turn. **Rows 2-9** *Sc in next ch-5 lp, ch 5; rep from *, end sc in last st. Ch 5, turn. After row 9 is completed, ch 1, turn. **Row 10 (RS)** Work 5 sc in each ch-5 lp across. Fasten off.

FINISHING

Block piece to measurements.

Beaded trim

With RS facing, join yarn with a sl st in last edging st sk on row 1 of ruffle. Working from left to right and in sk sts of row 1 of ruffle, work as foll: hdc in same st, ch 1, *hdc in next sk st, ch 1; rep from * across each side edge, end hdc in last sk st. Fasten off.

In the Bag

for intermediate crocheters

Tote your favorite beachside gear in a beguiling crocheted carry-all designed by Mari Lynn Patrick. It spotlights single crochet gussets with delicate "Irish Crochet" flowers joined by a chain mesh stitch. "In the Bag" first appeared in the Spring/Summer '03 issue of *Family Circle Easy Knitting* magazine.

MATERIALS

- *Lustersheen* by J&P Coats®, 1³/₄oz/50g balls, each approx 150yd/138m (cotton)
  1 ball each in #129 lilac (A-1), #206 pink (A-2) and #615 green (B)
  2 balls in #1 white(C)
- Size B/1 (2mm) crochet hook OR SIZE TO OBTAIN GAUGE
- Plastic handles by Judi & Co.
- ¹/₄yd/.25m of ¹/₂"/13m wide ribbon

FINISHED MEASUREMENTS

- Bag measures 9³/₄"/25cm square.

GAUGE

One flower motif is 3¹/₄"/8.25cm square.
TAKE TIME TO CHECK YOUR GAUGE.

MOTIF

Make 9 motifs using A-1 and 9 motifs using A-2. With A, ch 8, join with a sl st to first ch to form ring. **Rnd 1** With A, ch 6, *1 dc in ring, ch 3; rep from * 4 times more, join with a sl st to 3rd ch of ch-6 (6 sps). **Rnd 2** With A, in each ch-3 sp work 1 sc, 1 hdc, 3 dc, 1 hdc and 1 sc (6 petals). **Rnd 3** With A, ch 7, *1 hdc inserting hook from back to front to back around post of first dc on row 1 for 1 back hdc, ch 5; rep from * 5 times more, end sl st in 2nd ch of ch-7 (7 ch lps). **Rnd 4** With A, in each ch-5 sp work 1 sc, 1 hdc, 5 dc, 1 hdc and 1 sc; end rnd with sl st to first sc. **Rnd 5** With A, ch 9, *1 back hdc in corresponding hdc on rnd 3, ch 7; rep from * 6 times more, end draw B through 2nd ch of ch-9. Cut A. **Rnd 6** With B, ch 1, *work 1 sc, 1 hdc, 7 dc, 1 hdc and 1 sc in first lp, ch 4, sc in next ch-7 lp, ch 4; rep from *, end by sl st with C in first sc. Cut B. **Rnd 7** With C, ch 1, sc in sc with joining, *[ch 4, 1 sc in 3rd ch from hook for picot] twice, ch 1, 1 sc in center of corner petal, [ch 4, 1 picot] twice, ch 1, sc through ch-4 loop in B and A loop underneath, [ch 4, 1 picot] twice, ch 1, 1 sc through ch-4 loop in B and A loop underneath; rep from *, end sl st in first sc. Fasten off.

Join squares

Note Join square alternating A-1 and A-2 squares as in photo. To join 2 squares with C, sc in corner of first square, ch 4, picot, ch 4, sc in opposite corner of second square; then working down the side, [ch 2, sc in first square side, ch 2, sc in opposite side of second square] twice, ch 1, sc in center of corner then ch 5 and sc into corner of 3rd square; join 2 sides of the first and 3rd squares tog as before. When joining 4th square, at the center point between the 4 squares, work ch 2, join with sl st to 3rd ch of ch 5, ch 2 and join to opposite square. Work 3 rows of 3 sets of alternating joined motifs each for front and back.

Gussets

Work into the back piece along the side edge, with C, work as foll: work 1 back sc (as for back hdc) into corner, * ch 5, 1 back sc behind next sc, in color C; rep from * 10 times to corner (bottoms of bag), ch 6, work 1 back sc in next sc in color C; then rep from * cont around lower edge and side edge as before, turn. **Row 1 (WS)** Ch 2, work 5 hdc in ch-6 loop, *[5 hdc in ch-5 loop] 9 times, dc, ch 1 and dc in corner; rep from * around, turn. **Row 2** Working into back loop only, ch 1, work 20 sc, 20 hdc, 16 dc, dc, ch 1 and dc in corner sp, 56 dc across lower edge of bag, dc, ch 1 and dc in corner sp, 16 dc, 20 hdc and 20 sc up other side, turn. **Row 3** Ch 1, working into front loops only, work 20 sc, 20 hdc, then dc to corner, dc in corner ch-1 sp, work dc across lower edge of bag, then work other side of back to correspond. Fasten off. Work front piece in same way. Then sl st front and back pieces tog from WS through the outside lps only.

Top facing

Work row 1 as for row 1 of gusset with back sc and ch-lps. **Row 2** Working into each ch-lp work * 5 hdc in first lp, 4 hdc in next lp; rep from * to end, turn. **Row 3** Ch 2, work 1 hdc in each hdc. Fasten off. Turn facing to WS and tack neatly in place. To attach handles, draw a 6"/15cm length of ribbon through the handle slits and sew to inside of gusset with ends hanging loose to inside.

Comforts of Home

Warm and wonderful accents brighten every room of the house.

Block Party

for intermediate crocheters

Work up a punchy patchwork of twisted loops, horseshoe cables, triple tucks, shell ripples and more. Squares are stitched separately in eye-popping colors, then pieced together with contrasting yarn. Designed by Gloria Tracy, "Block Party" first appeared in the Spring/Summer '01 issue of *Family Circle Easy Knitting* magazine.

MATERIALS

- *Creme Bruleé* by Knit one Crochet too, 1³⁄₄oz/50g balls, each approx 131yd/120m (wool)
  7 balls in #210 brick (A)
  3 balls each in #849 rust (B) #299 orange (C) and #235 plum (E)
  2 balls in #294 peach (D)
- Size H/8 (5mm) crochet hook OR SIZE TO OBTAIN GAUGE

FINISHED MEASUREMENTS

- 32" x 47"/81cm x 119cm

GAUGE

1 square to 6"/15.5cm using size H/8 (5mm) crochet hook.

TAKE TIME TO CHECK YOUR GAUGE.

STITCHES USED

Mesh stitch (1)

Each square is 21 sts by 20 rows.

Double single crochet stitch (dsc)

Insert hook from front to back into 2nd ch from hook, yo and pull through, yo and draw through 1 lp yo and draw through 2 lps. Ch 23.

Row 1 Skip 2 ch (counts as dsc), dsc into next st, *skip 1 ch, 2 dsc into next ch; rep from * to last 2 ch, skip 1 ch, 2 dsc into last ch, turn. **Row 2** Ch 2, dsc into first st, *skip 1 st, 2 dsc into next st; rep from * to last 2 sts, skip 1 st, 2 dsc into last st, turn.

Rep row 2 for mesh st.

Block stitch (2)

Each square is 22 sts by 16 rows.
Ch 23.

Row 1 Sc in 2nd ch from hook, *ch 2, skip 2 ch, sc in next ch; rep from * to end, turn. **Row 2** Ch 4 (counts as dc and 1 ch), *3 dc in ch-2 sp, ch 1; rep from * to last st, dc in last st, turn.

Row 3 Ch 1, sc in first ch-1 sp, *ch 2, sc in next ch-1 sp; rep from * to end, turn.
Rep rows 2 and 3 for block st.

Shell ripple (3)

Each square is 22 sts by 13 rows.
Ch 25.

Row 1 Dc in 4th ch from hook, ch 1, dc in same ch as previous st, skip 2 ch, *2 dc in next ch, ch 1, 2 dc in same ch, skip 2 ch, dc in next ch, ch 1, dc in same ch, skip 2 ch; rep from * to last 3 ch, skip 2 ch, dc in last ch, turn. **Row 2** Ch 3, *2 dc in ch-1 sp, ch 1, 2 dc in same ch-1 sp, dc in next ch-1 sp, ch 1, dc in same ch-1 sp; rep from * to last ch-1 sp, 2 dc in ch-1 sp, ch 1, 2 dc in same ch-1 sp, dc in top of t-ch, turn. **Row 3** Ch 3, *dc in ch-1 sp, ch 1, dc in same ch-1 sp, 2 dc in next ch-1 sp, ch 1, 2 dc in same ch-1 sp; rep from * to last ch-1 sp, dc in ch-1 sp, ch 1, sc in same ch-1 sp, dc in top of t-ch, turn.

Rep rows 2 and 3 for shell ripple, working last rows as foll: Ch 1, sk next dc, *sc in each of next dc, ch-1 sp and next dc, skip next dc; rep from * to last st, sc in last st.

Ridge stitch (4)

Each square is 24 sts by 15 rows. Ch 27.

Row 1 Insert hook in 2nd ch from hook and draw through lp, skip 1 ch, insert hook through next ch and draw through lp (3 lps on hook), [yo and draw through 2 lps] twice, *insert hook through horizontal crossbar of st just worked, yo and draw through lp, insert hook through next ch and draw through lp (3 lps on hook), [yo and draw through 2 lps] twice; rep from * to end, turn. **Row 2** Ch 3, work as for row 1, working into sts instead of chains. Rep row 2 for ridge st.

Triple tucks (5)

Each square is 22 sts by 33 rows Ch 23.

Row 1 Sc in 2nd ch from hook and in each ch to end, turn. **Row 2 (RS)** Ch 1, sc in each sc, turn. **Row 3** Ch 4 (counts as 1 tr), tr in back lp of 2nd sc and in back lp of each sc to end, turn. **Row 4** Ch 1, *sc in back lp of each tr and in back lp of corresponding sc in row below; rep from *, end last st in top of t-ch, turn. **Row 5** Ch 1, sc in each sc, turn, Rep rows 2-5 for triple tucks.

Twisted loops (6)

Each square is 20 sts (19 lps) by 23 rows.
Ch 23.

Row 1 Sk 3 ch (counts as dc), dc in each ch to end, turn. **Row 2** *Ch 7, beg in 2nd st, sl st in back lp only, inserting hook from back to front; rep from *, end ch 7, sl st in top of t-ch,

(Continued on page 137)

Star Struck
for beginner crocheters

With all its different colors, Margarita Mejia's stellar throw would work in most any room. Single crochet the star-motif blocks, then trim with a striking black border; picot edging adds the final touch. "Star Struck" first appeared in the Spring/Summer '02 issue of *Family Circle Easy Knitting* magazine.

MATERIALS

- *TLC* by Red Heart®/Coats & Clark™, 5oz/140g balls, each approx 253yd/231m (acrylic)
  - 3 balls in #5335 sand (A)
  - 2 balls each in #5587 purple (B), #5657 kiwi (C), #5730 coral rose (D) and #5012 black (E)
  - 1 ball each in #5289 copper (F), #5585 lavender (G), #5662 spruce ((H), #5644 amber (I) and #5556 plum (J)
- Size H/8 (5mm) crochet hook OR SIZE TO OBTAIN GAUGE

FINISHED MEASUREMENTS

- 37"/94cm x 62"/157.5cm

GAUGE

One block to 7"/18cm-wide x 6¼"/16cm-high using size H/8 (5mm) crochet hook.
TAKE TIME TO CHECK YOUR GAUGE.

Notes

1 When changing color, draw new color through 2 lps on hook to complete sc.

2 Work sc sts over color that's being carried across WS of work to prevent loose strands. Make sure to maintain gauge.

3 To join yarn with a sc, make a lp and slip onto hook. Insert hook into st. Yo and draw up a lp. Yo and draw through 2 lps on hook.

STAR BLOCK

Make 40 blocks foll placement diagram for background and star colorways. With background color, ch 28.

Row 1 (RS) Sc in 2nd ch from hook and in each ch across—27 sts. Ch 1, turn. **Row 2** Sc in each st across. Ch 1, turn. Rep row 2 for pat st.

Beg chart

Beg on row 3 (RS) and work even to chart row 27. Fasten off.

Edging

From RS, join E with a sc in top right corner. **Rnd 1** [Ch 1, sk next st, sc in next st] 12 times, ch 1, in next corner work (sc, ch 2, sc), turn to side edge. [Ch 1, sk next row, sc in side edge of next row] 12 times, ch 1, in next corner work (sc, ch 2, sc), turn to bottom edge. Working between sts, [ch 1, sk next st, sc between next 2 sts] 12 times, ch 1, in next corner work (sc, ch 2, sc), turn to side edge. [Ch 1, sk next row, sc in side edge of next row] 12 times, end ch 1, sc in last corner, ch 2. Join rnd with a sl st in first sc. Fasten off.

FINISHING

With E, sew squares tog foll placement diagram.

Border

Rnd 1 Join A with a sc in any corner ch-2 sp, ch 2, sc in same sp (first corner made), ch 1, ** *sc in next ch-1 sp, ch 1; rep from * to next corner, work (sc, ch 2, sc) in corner ch-2 sp, ch 1; rep from ** around to first corner, join rnd with a sl st in first sc. **Rnds 2-8** Ch 1, work (sc, ch 2, sc) in first corner, ch 1, ** *sc in next ch-1 sp, ch 1; rep from * to next corner, work (sc, ch 2, sc) in corner ch-2 sp, ch 1; rep from ** around to first corner, join rnd with a sl st in ch-1. **Rnd 9** Ch 1, work (sc, ch 2, sc) in first corner, *sc in next ch-1 sp, (ch 3, sc in 3rd ch from hook—picot made), sc in next ch-1 sp; rep from * around working (sc, ch 2, sc) in each corner ch-2 sp, join rnd with a sl st in ch-1. Fasten off.

(See diagrams on page 138)

Diamond Jubilee

for beginner crocheters

Single-crochet squares, bold black border and captivating diamond motifs make this cozy coverlet a true gem. Designed by Margarita Mejia, it's inspired by a country quilt. "Diamond Jubilee" first appeared in the Spring/Summer '02 issue of *Family Circle Easy Knitting* magazine.

MATERIALS

- *Red Heart® Classic* by Red Heart®/Coats & Clark™, 3½oz/100g skeins, each approx 198yd/181m (acrylic)
  4 skeins in #12 black (A)
  2 skeins each in #827 lt periwinkle (B), #508 peacock green (C), #676 emerald green (D), #822 true blue (E), #686 paddy green (F), #513 parakeet (G) and #848 skipper blue (H)
- Size H/8 (5mm) crochet hook OR SIZE TO OBTAIN GAUGE

FINISHED MEASUREMENTS

- 40½"/103cm x 59½"/151cm

GAUGE

One block to 7"/18cm-wide by 6 1/4"/16cm-high using size H/8 (5mm) crochet hook. TAKE TIME TO CHECK YOUR GAUGE.

Notes

1 When changing color, draw new color through 2 lps on hook to complete sc.

2 Do not carry colors across, use a separate strand of yarn for each color section.

3 To join yarn with a sc, make a lp and slip onto hook. Insert hook into sp. Yo and draw up a lp. Yo and draw through 2 lps on hook.

DIAMOND BLOCK

Make 40 blocks foll placement diagram for background and diamond colorways. With background color, ch 28.

Row 1 (RS) Sc in 2nd ch from hook and in each ch across—27 sts. Ch 1, turn. **Row 2** Sc in each st across. Ch 1, turn. Rep row 2 for pat st.

Beg chart

Beg on row 3 (RS) and work even to chart row 27. Fasten off.

Edging

Rnd 1 From RS, join A with a sc in top right corner. Sc in next 25 sts, work (sc, ch 2, sc) in next corner. Turn to side edge and work 25 sc evenly spaced to next corner, work (sc, ch 2, sc) in corner. Turn to bottom edge. Working between sts, work 25 sc evenly spaced across bottom edge to next corner, work (sc, ch 2, sc) in corner. Turn to side edge and work 25 sc evenly spaced to first corner, work (sc, ch 2) in corner, join rnd with a sl st in first sc. Fasten off.

FINISHING

With A, sew squares tog foll placement diagram.

Border

Rnd 1 From RS, join A with a sc in any corner ch-2 sp, ch 1, ** *sc in next st, ch 1, sk next st; rep from * to next corner ch-2 sp, work (sc, ch 2, sc) in corner; rep from ** to first corner, end ch 2, join rnd with a sl st in first sc. Fasten off. **Rnd 2** From RS, join G with a sc in any corner ch-2 sp, ch 1, ** *sc in next ch-1 sp, ch 1; rep from * to next corner, work (sc, ch 2, sc) in corner ch-2 sp, ch 1: rep from ** around to first corner, end ch 2, join rnd with a sl st in first sc. Fasten off. **Rnd 3** With D, rep rnd 2. **Rnd 4** With C, rep rnd 2. **Rnd 5** With E, rep rnd 2. **Rnd 6** With F, rep rnd 2. **Rnd 7** With B, rep rnd 2. **Rnd 8** With H, rep rnd 2. **Rnd 9** From RS, join A with a sl st in any corner ch-2 sp, ** *(sc, ch 3, dc) in next ch-1sp, sk next sp; rep from * to next corner, work (sc, ch 3, 2 dc) in corner ch-2 sp; rep from ** around to first corner, join rnd with a sl st in first sc. Fasten off.

(See diagrams on page 137)

Romantic Notion

for intermediate crocheters

An exquisite border of delicate crocheted lace adds old-fashioned elegance to plain pillows. Designed by Jacquelyn Smyth, "Romantic Notion" first appeared in the Spring/Summer '99 issue of *Family Circle Easy Knitting* magazine.

MATERIALS

- *Coats "Opera"* by Patons®/Coats Patons®, 1³⁄₄oz/ 50g ball approx 249yd/230m (cotton)

12" pillow
- 1 ball in #500 white
- Pillow form, 12"/30.5cm square

16" pillow
- 1 ball in #500 white
- Pillow form, 16"/40.5cm square

Both pillows
- Size 6 (1.5mm) steel crochet hook OR SIZE TO OBTAIN GAUGE
- Lavender damask fabric ¹⁄₂ yd/.5m
- 3 snaps
- Matching thread
- Spray starch

FINISHED MEASUREMENTS

- 12"/30.5cm x 16"/40.5cm

GAUGES

12" pillow
- Edging is approx 2"/5cm wide using steel crochet hook size 6 (1.5mm).

16" pillow
- Edging is approx 1¹⁄₄"/3cm wide using steel crochet hook size 6 (1.5mm).

TAKE TIME TO CHECK YOUR GAUGES.

12"/30.5cm PILLOW

Lace Edging

Beg at narrow end, ch 11.

Row 1 (3 dc, ch 2, dc) in 7th ch from hook, *sk 1 ch, (3 dc, ch 2, dc) in next ch; rep from * twice. Ch 6, turn.

Row 2 *(3 dc, ch 2, dc) in next ch-2 sp; rep from * twice. Ch 6, turn.

Rep row 2 until piece measures approx 52"/132cm from beg, do not turn at end of last row.

Heading

Working across adjacent long edge, ch 1, sc in same lp, *ch 5, sc in next ch-6 lp; rep from *. Fasten off. Spray edging with spray starch and press, using a press cloth.

PILLOW

From fabric, cut a 13"/33cm square and 2 pieces each 9"/22.5cm x 13"/33cm for pillow back. Press one long edge on each backing piece 1"/2.5cm twice to the WS. Overlap backing pieces to form a 13"/33cm square and baste lapped edges. With RS of back and front tog, sew around all sides using a ¹⁄₂"/1.25cm seam. Turn right side out and press. Top stitch around pillow, ¹⁄₄"/.6cm from edge. Sew 3 snaps inside lapped back opening. Pin edging around square, pleating slightly at each corner. Sew ends of edging tog. By hand, sew edging to pillow.

16"/40.5cm PILLOW

Lace Edging

Make a ch slightly longer than outside edge of pillow, plus approx 4"/10cm to allow for corners.

Row 1 Sc in 2nd ch from hook and in each ch across having a number of sc divisible by 16 plus 8 extra. Cut off rem ch. Ch 4, turn. **Row 2** Holding back on hook last lp of each tr, tr in next 3 sc, yo and through all lps on hook—beg cluster made; *ch 3, holding back on hook last lp of each tr, tr in next 4 sc, yo and through all lps on hook—cluster made; rep from * across. Ch 1, turn. **Row 3** Sl st in next sp, ch 1, sc in same sp, *ch 1, skip next sp, ([dtr, ch 1] 8 times, dtr) in next sp, ch 1, skip next sp, sc in next sp; rep from * across, sl st to tip of last cluster. Ch 5, turn. **Row 4** Ch 1, sc in next sp, sc in next sc, *(ch 1, sc) 9 times in next sp, ch 1, sc in sp, sc in sc, sc in sp; rep from *. Fasten off. Spray edging with spray starch and press, using a press cloth.

PILLOW

From fabric, cut a 17"/43cm square and 2 pieces each 11"/27.5cm x 17"/43cm for pillow back. Make pillow and sew on edging as for smaller pillow.

Table Manners

Stitch a crochet trim to a store-bought tablecloth and voilà—instant heirloom! Jacquelyn Smyth's ultra-easy accent is a perfect beginner project. "Table Manners" first appeared in the Spring/Summer '99 issue of *Family Circle Easy Knitting* magazine.

MATERIALS
- *Traditions* by DMC, 2.3oz/65g balls each approx 400yd/365m (cotton)
  2 ball in #5211 lilac
- Size B/1 (2mm) crochet hook OR SIZE TO OBTAIN GAUGE
- 1¼yd (1.4m) lavender floral fabric for topper
- Lavender fabric as specified on Butterick pattern # 3341, View D for underskirt
- Matching thread
- Spray starch

FINISHED MEASUREMENTS
- Topper is 44"/111.5cm square

GAUGE
Edging is approx 2"/5cm wide using size B/1 (2mm) hook.
TAKE TIME TO CHECK YOUR GAUGE.

LACE EDGING
Beg at narrow end, ch 11.
Row 1 (3 dc, ch 2, dc) in 7th ch from hook; sk 1 ch, (3 dc, ch 2, dc) in next ch; rep from *. Ch 6, turn.
Row 2 *(3 dc, ch 2, dc) in next ch-2 sp; rep from *. Ch 6, turn. Rep row 2 until piece measures approx 180"/457cm from beg, do not turn at end of last row.

Heading
Working across adjacent long edge, ch 1, sc in same lp, *ch 5, sc in ch-6 lp; rep from *. Fasten off. Spray edging with spray starch and press, using a press cloth.

Table Topper
Press ¼"/.6cm hem twice to RS of floral fabric and sew in place. By hand, backstitch heading of crochet edging over hem. Press topper on WS.

Underskirt
Follow pattern instructions for view D.

Window Dressing

for intermediate crocheters

Pretty up a plain-Jane valance with some luscious lace trim. Crochet to the length needed and stitch to the fabric for a quick and easy change of view. Designed by Jacquelyn Smyth, "Window Dressing" first appeared in the Spring/Summer '99 issue of *Family Circle Easy Knitting* magazine.

MATERIALS

- *South Maid® Cotton Crochet Thread* by Coats & Clark™, 2½oz/70g each approx 400yd/365m (cotton)
  1 ball of #001 white
- Size 6 (1.75mm) steel crochet hook OR SIZE TO OBTAIN GAUGE
- Lavender floral fabric for valance, yardage as specified in Butterick pattern #6434, View C
- Matching and white sewing threads
- Spray starch

GAUGE

Edging is approx 1½"/4cm wide using steel crochet hook size 6 (1.75mm).
TAKE TIME TO CHECK YOUR GAUGE.

Note

Construct valance following pattern directions for View C.

LACE EDGING

Beg at narrow end, ch 9.
Row 1 Dc in 8th ch from hook; ch 2, dc in same ch, ch 2, (dc, ch 2, dc) in last ch. Ch 5, turn.
Row 2 Dc in center ch-2 sp, (ch 2, dc) 3 times in same sp. Ch 5, turn. Rep row 2 until piece measures same length as lower, curved edge of valance, at end of last row, ch 3, do not turn.

Heading

Working across adjacent long edge, *work 2 sc in 5-ch loop, ch 4; rep from * across to opposite end of edging. Sl st along narrow end.

Lower edge

Working across remaining long edge, work 9 dc in each ch-5 loop. Fasten off. Spray edging with spray starch and press, using a press cloth. By hand, with white thread, backstitch heading of crochet edging along curved edge of valance.

Graphic Art
for intermediate crocheters

Crochet goes contemporary in Margarita Mejia's boldly patterned blanket and pillow set. Afghan squares are worked in the round in three colors, stitched together and finished off with a single crochet border. The cross pillow is stitched in single crochet; its mates are worked in the round. "Graphic Art" first appeared in the Fall '02 issue of *Family Circle Easy Knitting* magazine.

MATERIALS
■ *Velvet Touch* by Wendy/Berroco, Inc. 1³/₄oz/50g skeins, each approx 114yd/104m (polyamide)

Afghan
- 2 skeins in #1202 red (A)
- 8 skeins in #2007 black (B)
- 7 skeins in #1200 white (C)

■ Size H/8 (5mm) crochet hook OR SIZE TO OBTAIN GAUGE

Cross pillow
- 2 skeins each in #1200 white (A) and #1202 red (B)

Two-Color Square pillow
- 2 skeins in #1200 white (A)
- 4 skeins in #1202 red (B)

Three-Color Square pillow
- 1 skein in #1202 red (A)
- 2 skeins each in #1200 white (B) and #2007 black (C)

For all pillows
■ Size H/8 (5mm) crochet hook OR SIZE TO OBTAIN GAUGE
■ 18"/46cm x 18"/46cm pillow form

FINISHED MEASUREMENTS
Afghan
■ 44¹/₄" x 44¹/₄"/112 x 112cm
For all pillows
■ 18" x 18"/46 x 46cm

GAUGES
Afghan
One square to 8¹/₄"/21cm using size H/8 (5mm) crochet hook.
For all pillows
14 sts and 15 rows to 4"/10cm over sc using size H/8 (5mm) crochet hook.
TAKE TIME TO CHECK YOUR GAUGE.

Note
To join rnd and change color, insert hook into ch-1, then draw new color through all lps on hook.

AFGHAN

SQUARE
(make 25)
With A, ch 4. Join ch with a sl st forming a ring. **Rnd 1** Ch 3 (counts as 1 sc and ch 2), *sc over ring, ch 2 (corner sp); rep from * around 3 times. Join rnd with a sl st in 1st ch of ch-3. **Rnd 2** Ch 1, *work [sc, ch 2, sc] in next corner ch-2 sp, sc in next sc; rep from * around 3 times, end [sc, ch 2, sc] in next corner ch-2 sp. Join rnd with a sl st in ch-1. **Rnd 3** Ch 1, *work [sc, ch 2, sc] in next corner ch-2 sp, sc in next 3 sc; rep from * around 3 times, end [sc, ch 2, sc] in next corner ch-2 sp, sc in next 2 sc. Join rnd with a sl st in ch-1. **Rnd 4** Ch 1, *work [sc, ch 2, sc] in next corner ch-2 sp, sc in next 5 sc; rep from * around 3 times, end [sc, ch 2, sc] in next corner ch-2 sp, sc in next 4 sc. Join rnd with a sl st in ch-1. **Rnd 5** Ch 1, *work [sc, ch 2, sc] in next corner ch-2 sp, sc in next 7 sc; rep from * around 3 times, end [sc, ch 2, sc] in next corner ch-2 sp, sc in next 6 sc. Join rnd with a sl st in ch-1, changing to B. **Rnds 6-12** Cont to work 2 more sc between each corner every rnd. On rnd 12, there are 21 sc between corners and change to C at end of this rnd. **Rnds 13-15** Cont to work 2 more sc between each corner every rnd. On rnd 15, there are 27 sc between corners. Fasten off.

FINISHING
With C, sew 5 squares tog forming 5 strips. Sew strips tog to form afghan.

Edging
From RS, join C with a sl st 1 st before any ch-2 corner sp. **Rnds 1-3** Ch 1, *work [sc, ch 2, sc] in next corner ch-2 sp, sc in each sc to next corner; rep from * around, end [sc, ch 2, sc] in next corner ch-2 sp, sc in next 26 sc. Join rnd with a sl st in ch-1. After rnd 3 is completed, join rnd

(Continued on page 138)

Heart Warming

for intermediate crocheters

Tunisian crochet and sculptural stitches assure that this charming pillow is a delightful room accent. Fast and fun to stitch, it makes a wonderful gift. "Heart Warming" first appeared in the Holiday '02 issue of *Family Circle Easy Knitting* magazine.

MATERIALS

▓ *TLC* by Coats & Clark™, 5oz/140g skeins, each approx 253yd/233m (acrylic)
6 skeins #5017 ecru
▓ Size H/8 (5mm) afghan hook OR SIZE TO OBTAIN GAUGE
▓ Size H/8 (5mm) crochet hook
▓ Two 16"/40.5 cm x 18"/46cm pieces of polyester batting
▓ One bag polyester fiberfill

FINISHED MEASUREMENTS

▓ 16" x 18"/40.5 x 46cm

GAUGE

18 sts and 15 rows to 4"/10cm over basic afghan st using size H/8 (5mm) afghan hook. TAKE TIME TO CHECK YOUR GAUGE.

BASIC AFGHAN STITCH

First half

Working from right to left, draw up a lp in each vertical thread, retaining all lps on hook.

Second half

Working from left to right, yo and draw through next 2 lps on hook to the end.

Notes

1 Each row of basic afghan st is worked in two halves. The first half is worked from right to left and the second half is worked from left to right.

2 Each row on chart represents both first and second halves.

3 Each vertical line on chart represents one vertical thread.

4 Always count the amount of lps you have on the hook after you have worked the first half of row to make sure you have the correct amount.

BACK

With afghan hook, ch 74. Refer to Basic Afghan Stitch. **Row 1 (first half)** Working through back lps of ch, insert hook into 2nd ch from hook, yo and draw up a lp. Retaining all lps on hook, draw up a lp in each ch to end—74 lps on hook. **Row 1 (second half)** Yo, draw through 1 lp, *yo and draw through next 2 lps on hook; rep from * to end. **Row 2 (first half)** Insert hook under 2nd vertical thread from side edge of the previous row. Yo and draw up a lp. Retaining all lps on hook, draw up a lp in each vertical thread to end. **Row 2 (second half)** Yo, draw through 1 lp, *yo and draw through next 2 lps on hook; rep from * to end. Rep row 2 until 76 rows have been completed. Fasten off.

FRONT SQUARE

(make 4)

With afghan hook, ch 37. Work as for back until 4 rows have been completed.

Beg chart

Row 5 (first half) Draw up a lp in first 2 vertical threads—3 lps on hook. Yo, insert hook under 2nd vertical thread of 3 rows below, yo and draw up a lp, yo and draw through 2 lps on hook (first raised dc made). Work another raised dc under same vertical thread. Yo and draw through 2 lps on hook (double raised dc made)—4 lps on hook. Sk next 3 vertical threads of 3 rows below and work a double raised dc—5 lps on hook. These 2 double raised dc replace the 2 unworked sts behind them. *Draw up a lp in each of next 3 vertical threads, work double raised dc under vertical thread next to previous double raised dc, sk next 3 vertical threads of 3 rows below, work double raised dc under next vertical thread; rep from *, end draw up a lp in last 2 vertical threads. **Row 5 (second half)** Yo, draw through 1 lp, *yo and draw through next 2 lps on hook; rep from * to end. **Row 6 (first half)** Insert hook under 2nd vertical thread from side edge of the previous row. Yo and draw up a lp. Retaining all lps on hook, draw up a lp in each vertical thread to end. **Row 6 (second half)** Rep second half of row 5. **Row 7 (first half)** Draw up a lp in first 2 vertical threads. Work double raised dc under 2nd vertical thread of 3 rows below, sk next 3 vertical threads of 3 rows below, work double raised dc under next vertical thread. Draw up a lp in next 28 vertical threads. Work double raised dc under 6th vertical thread (from LH edge) of 3 rows below, sk

(Continued on page 139)

The Great Indoors

Bring the wonder of nature into your home with this beautiful blanket designed by Margarita Mejia. Squares are crocheted individually and then joined together, making this the perfect portable project. Finish the edged with a two-color shell stitch. "The Great Indoors" first appeared in the Holiday '02 issue of *Family Circle Easy Knitting* magazine.

MATERIALS

- *Imagine* by Lion Brand Yarn Company, 2.7oz/70g skeins, each approx 222yd/203m (acrylic/mohair)
  7 skeins #099 fisherman (MC)
  4 skeins #173 pine (B)
  2 skeins #126 brown (A)
- Size J/10 (6mm) crochet hook OR SIZE TO OBTAIN GAUGE

FINISHED MEASUREMENTS

- 48" x 63"/122 x 160cm

GAUGE

One square to 9"/23cm; 12 sts and 12 rows to 4"/10cm using size J/10 (6mm) crochet hook. TAKE TIME TO CHECK YOUR GAUGE.

Notes

1 When changing color, draw new color through 2 lps on hook to complete sc.

2 Work sts over color that's being carried across WS of work to prevent loose strands. Make sure to maintain gauge.

3 To dec 1 sc, [insert hook into next st and draw up a lp] twice, yo and draw through all 3 lps on hook.

SQUARE

(make 18)

With MC, ch 2. **Row 1 (RS)** Sc in 2nd ch from hook—1 st. Ch 1, turn. **Row 2** Work 3 sc in st. Ch 1, turn. **Row 3** Work 2 sc in first st, sc in next st, work 2 sc in last st—5 sts. Ch 1, turn. **Row 4** Work 2 sc in first st, sc in next 3 sts, work 2 sc in last st—7 sts. Ch 1, turn.

Beg chart pat

Row 5 (RS) Work 2 sc in first st, sc in next st, beg chart with st 10 and work to st 12, with A, sc in next st, work 2 sc in last st—9 sts. Ch 1, turn. Cont to in this way, AT SAME TIME, cont to

inc 1 st each side every row until row 19 is completed (37 sts), then dec 1 st each side every row until 3 sts rem. Last row [Insert hook into next st and draw up a lp] 3 times, yo and draw through all 4 lps on hook—1 st. Ch 1, turn to side edge.

Edging

With RS facing, work 1 sc in each row around and work 3 sc in each corner; make sure work lies flat. Join rnd with a sl st in ch-1. Fasten off.

HALF SQUARE 1

(make 4)

With MC, ch 2. **Row 1 (WS)** Sc in 2nd ch from hook—1 st. Ch 1, turn. **Row 2** Work 3 sc in st. Ch 1, turn. **Row 3** Work 2 sc in first st, sc in next st, work 2 sc in last st—5 sts. Ch 1, turn. Cont to inc 1 st each side every row until 19 rows have been completed—37 sts. Ch 1, turn to side edge.

Edging

With RS facing, work 1 sc in each row around and work 3 sc in each corner; make sure work lies flat. Join rnd with a sl st in ch-1. Fasten off.

HALF SQUARE 2

(make 6)

With MC, ch 2. **Row 1 (WS)** Sc in 2nd ch from hook—1 st. Ch 1, turn. **Row 2** Work 2 sc in st. Ch 1, turn. **Row 3** Work 2 sc in first st, sc in last st—

3 sts. Ch 1, turn. **Row 4** Sc in first 2 sts, work 2 sc in last st—4 sts. Ch 1, turn. Cont to inc 1 st at same edge until 19 rows have been completed (19 sts), then dec 1 st at same edge every row until 1 st rem. Ch 1, turn to side edge. Work edging as for half square 1.

QUARTER SQUARE 3

(make 4)

Work as for half square 2 until row 19 is completed—19 sts. Ch 1, turn to side edge. Work edging as for half square 1.

FINISHING

With MC, whip-stitch pieces tog foll placement diagram.

Border

Rnd 1 Join A with a sl st in any corner st, ch 3 (counts as 1 dc), work 2 dc in same st (half corner made), ch 1, sk next 2 sts, ** +work 3 dc in next st, ch 1, sk next 2 sts; rep from + to next corner st, work (3 dc, ch 2, 3 dc) in same st (corner made); rep from ** around to beg half corner, end work 3 dc in same st as half corner, ch 2. Join rnd with a sl st in 3rd ch of ch-3. Fasten off. **Rnd 2** Join B with a sl st in any corner ch-2 sp, ch 3, work 2 dc in same sp, ch 1, ** +work 3 dc in next ch-1 sp, ch 1; rep from + to next corner ch-2 sp, work (3 dc, ch 2, 3 dc) in same sp; rep from ** around to beg half corner,

(Continued on page 140)

True Blue

for intermediate crocheters

Serene squares of blue lend a soothing note to any room. The cool country check pattern takes its cue from old-fashioned patchwork quilts. Designed by Katherine Eng, "True Blue" first appeared in the Fall '94 issue of *Family Circle Knitting* magazine.

MATERIALS

▧ *Supersaver Red Heart*® by Coats and Clark™, 8oz/227g balls, each approx 452yd/411m (acrylic)
   3 balls in #387 navy (A)
   2 balls in #382 blue (B)
   I ball in #380 light blue (C)
▧ Size J/10 (6.00mm) crochet hook, OR SIZE TO OBTAIN GAUGE

FINISHED MEASUREMENTS
▧ 48 x 65"/122cm x 165cm

GAUGE

12 sts to 4"/10cm and 20 rows to 5"/ 9.5cm in single crochet using size J/10 (6.00mm) crochet hook.

Center motif and each rem square measures 33/4"/9.5cm across using size J/ 10 (6.00mm) crochet hook.

TAKE TIME TO CHECK YOUR GAUGE.

CENTER MOTIF (CM)

With hook and A, ch 4. Join with sl st to form ring. Ch 1.

Rnd 1 *Sc into ring, ch 2; rep from * 6 times, end sc into ring, hdc to beg sc. Ch 1.

Rnd 2 Work (sc, ch 2, sc) in ch-2 sp, *ch 1, sc in next ch-2 sp, ch 1, work (sc, ch 2, sc) in next ch-2 sp; rep from * twice, end ch 1, sc in next sp, st st to beg sc. SI st along edge to ch-2 sp. Ch 1.

Rnd 3 Sc in same ch-2 sp, *ch 1, skip sc and ch-1 sp, work (2 dc, ch 2, 2 dc) in next sc, ch 1, sc in corner ch-2 sp; rep from * 3 times, end last rep ch 1, sl st to beg sc. Ch 1.

Rnd 4 Work 10 sc along each side as foil: work I sc in each ch-1 sp and dc, 2 scs in each sc and work (sc, ch 2, sc) in each corner ch-2 sp. Join with sl st to beg ch. Fasten off.

First rnd (S1-S4)

S1 With RS of center motif facing and A, join yarn to any corner ch-2 sp. Ch 12.

Row 1 (RS) Sc in 2nd ch from hook, *ch 1, skip I ch, sc in next ch; rep from * 4 times-6 scs and 5 ch-1 sps. SI st in first sc at side edge of center motif, then in 2nd sc. Ch 1, turn at end of this and all foll rows.

Row 2 (WS) Sc in first sc, *ch 1, skip next ch-1 sp, sc in next sc; rep from * across.

Row 3 Rep row 2, working sl st in 3rd, then 4th sc at side edge of center motif.

Rows 4-11 Rep row 2, working st st in 5th and 6th sc (row 5), 7th and 8th sc (row 7) and 9th and 10th sc (row 9). On row 11, sl st into ch-2 sp * Do not fasten off. S2 Ch 12. Rep rows I11 of St. In same way, work S3 and S4.

2nd rnd (S5-S12)

S5 With 13, join yarn to 11th foundation ch of St. Ch 12. Rep rows 1-11 of St. Do not fasten off. S6 Work square on top of square as fell: *Ch 1, skip I sc, sc in next sc; rep from * 4 times-6 scs and 5 ch-1 sps. SI st in first sc at side edge of adjoining motif (S2), then in 2nd sc. Ch 1, turn at end of this and all foll rows. Rep rows 2-11 of S 1. S7 Ch 12. Work rows 1 -11 of St. S8 Ch 1. Work square on top of square by rep S6, working across side of S2. S9 Rep ST S10 Ch 1. Rep S6, working across side of S3. S11 Ch 12. Rep ST S12 Ch 1. Rep S6, working across side of S4.

Partial rnd 6

Join A to upper right corner of first square of 5th rnd, ch 1 and, working square on top of square as before, work around half of piece. In same way, join A and complete 2nd half.

Partial rnd 7

Join B to upper right corner of first square of last rnd. Complete as for partial rnd 6. Length established-15 squares long.

Work across sides

Partial rnd 8 With C, work 5 squares across each side edge. **Partial rnd 9** With B, work 4 squares across each side edge ' **Partial rnd 10** With A, work 3 squares across each side edge. **Partial rnd 11** With A, work 2 squares across each side edge.

CORNER SQUARES

With B, work final 4 corner squares.

BORDER

With RS facing, join A to corner and work 169 sc along length of piece. Ch 1, turn.

Row 1 Sc in first sc, *skip 2 sc, work (2 dc, ch 2, 2 de) in next sc (shell made), skip 2 sc, sc in next sc; rep from *. Ch 1, turn.

Row 2 Sc in first sc, *ch 2, (sc, ch 2, sc) in ch-2 sp,

(Continued on page 139)

Kid Stuff

Stitch up some fun for toddlers, tweens and teens.

Neutral Zone

for intermediate crocheters

East meets West in Sharon Valiant's hippie-chic cardigan. Featuring kimono-styled sleeves and single-crochet edging, it's the perfect partern for jeans and a tee. "Neutral Zone" first appeared in the Spring/Summer '01 issue of *Family Circle Easy Knitting* magazine.

MATERIALS

■ *Microspun* by Lion Brand Yarn Co., 2½oz/70g balls, each approx 168yd/154m (acrylic)

   7 (8) balls in #124 mocha (A)

   5 (6) balls in #98 vanilla (B)

■ Size H/8 (5mm) crochet hook for size Small/Medium OR SIZE TO OBTAIN GAUGE

■ Size I/9 (5.5mm) crochet hook for size Large OR SIZE TO OBTAIN GAUGE

SIZES

Sized for Small/Medium (Large). Shown in size Small/Medium.

FINISHED MEASUREMENTS

■ Bust 40 (42½)"/101.5 (108)cm

■ Length 24½ (26)"/62 (66)cm

■ Upper arm 20 (21¼)"/51 (54)cm

GAUGES

■ Square for size Small/Medium measures 4"/10cm using size H/8 (5mm) hook

■ Square for size Large measures 4µ"/11cm using size I/9 (5.5mm) hook.

TAKE TIME TO CHECK YOUR GAUGE

Note

When changing colors, bring new color under old color and use new color as last yo on hook to complete last st in old color.

SQUARE

(make 106)

Beg at center with appropriate hook for chosen size, with A, ch 8, join with a sl st to first ch to form ring. **Rnd 1** Ch 1, work 16 sc in ring, insert hook in first sc to join and with B, yo hook and draw through sc to complete joining. Drop A to WS and turn work. **Rnd 2 (WS)** With B, ch 3 (counts as first dc), in same st work 1 dc, ch 2, 2 dc, *skip 1 sc, in next sc work 2 dc, ch 2 and 2 dc; rep from * around, join with sl st

to top of ch-3, sl st across to next ch-2 sp, pulling through A on last yo, turn. **Rnd 3 (RS)** With A, *sc in ch-2 sp, ch 1, in next ch-2 sp work 3 tr, ch 2 and 3 tr for corner, ch 1, rep from * around, join with sl st to first sc. **Rnd 4** Note Corners are worked with B and straight sides are worked with A. To beg rnd, pick up B and then carry B loosely across top of previous rnd while working. With A, *1 sc in each of 3 tr on 2nd half of a corner, sc in next ch-1 sp, sc in next sc, sc in next ch-1 sp, pick up B on last yo, work 2 sc, ch 2 and 2 sc in corner ch-2 sp, pick up A on last yo; rep from * around. Fasten off.

FINISHING

Foll diagram using matching color and working through back lps only, sew 56 squares tog to form back and fronts. Fold at fold lines for side seams and join A to A and B to B for shoulders.

SLEEVES

Sew tog 25 squares for each sleeve foll diagram. Fold sleeve in half at fold line for underarm seam and join to armhole openings.

Borders

Rnd 1 With A, join at center back neck, *(ch 1, skip 1 sc, sc in next sc) to 2 sc before center shoulder seam, 2 dc in shoulder seam, skip 2 sc (sc in next sc, ch 1, skip 1 sc) to front corner, in corner work 1 sc, ch 2 and 1 sc, (ch 1, skip 1 sc,

sc in next sc) to next corner, rep from * around as established (working 2 dc in shoulder seam), end with a sl st to first sc to join rnd. **Rnd 2** Work as for rnd 1. Fasten off.

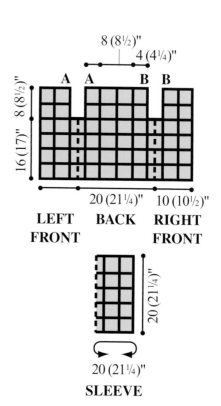

8 (8½)"

4 (4¼)"

A   A   B   B

8 (8½)"

16 (17)"

20 (21¼)"   10 (10½)"

LEFT FRONT   **BACK**   **RIGHT FRONT**

20 (21¼)"

20 (21¼)"

SLEEVE

Hat Trick

for advanced crocheters

Chase the chill with Lily Chin's Andean inspired topper. Warm and wooly, it boasts twisted cord ties, fringed edging and a fun pompom finish. "Hat Trick" first appeared in the Winter '99/'00 issue of *Family Circle Easy Knitting* magazine.

MATERIALS

- *Wool-Ease* by Lion Brand Yarn Co., 3oz/85g balls, each approx 197yd/179m (acrylic/wool)
  1 ball each in #153 black (A), #098 natural (B), #124 camel (C), #127 brown (D) and #151 grey heather (E)
- *Homespun*, 6oz/170g balls, each approx 185yd/169m (100% Acrilan® Acrylic)
  1 ball in #311 rococo (F)
- Sizes G/6 and H/8 (4.5 and 5mm) crochet hook OR SIZE TO OBTAIN GAUGE

FINISHED MEASUREMENTS

- Head circumference approx 21½"/54.5cm

GAUGE

18 dc or sc to 4"/10cm with larger hook.
TAKE TIME TO CHECK YOUR GAUGE.

Note

When changing colors, work off last lps of old-color-st with new color. Work over strand of color not in use to hide other color in checkerboard pat.

RIBBING

(worked from side-to-side)
With E and smaller hook, ch 7.
Row 1 Sc in 2nd ch from hook and in each ch across—6 sc. **Row 2** Ch 1 and turn, sc in first sc, sc into back lps of each next 4 sc, sc in last sc (through both lps). Rep row 2 for rib. Work until rib band measures snugly around head, approx 20"-21"/50.5cm-53.5cm, making sure there are an even number of rows. Fasten and end off leaving a 6"/15.5cm tail. With tail, sew ends tog to form a circle, being careful not to twist.

BODY

(worked from bottom up)
Welt
With A and larger hook, join to one side edge of rib and work 96 sc evenly around, join with sl st to first st.
Next row (WS) Ch 1 and turn, sc in each st around, join to beg, fasten and end off.

Large checkerboard pat
With RS facing and B, join to back lp of any st. Ch 3 (counts as a dc). Work into the back lp of each st, dc in each of next 5 sts, changing to D at last st, *with D, dc in each of next 6 sts, changing to B at last st, with B, dc in each of next 6 sts, changing to D at last st; rep from * around, end with 6 dc in D, join with sl st to top of beg ch-3. **Next rnd (WS)** With D, ch 3 (counts as a dc). Working through both lps of each st, dc in each of next 5 sts, changing to B at last st, *with B, dc in each of next 6 sts, changing to D at last st, with D, dc in each of next 6 sts, changing to B at last st; rep from * around, end with 6 dc in B and changing to D at last st, join with sl st to top of beg ch-3. **Next rnd (RS)** Rep last row to alternate colors, do not change to D at last st. **Next rnd (WS)** With B, ch 3 (counts as a dc), dc in next st, dec next 2 sts tog, dc in each of next 2 sts, changing to D at last st, *with D, dc in each of next 2 sts, dec next 2 dc tog, dc in each of next 2 sts, changing to B at last st, with B, dc in each of next 2 sts, dec next 2 dc tog, dc in each of next 2 sts, changing to D at last st; rep from *

around, end with dc in each of next 2 sts, dec next 2 dc tog, dc in each of next 2 sts in D, join with sl st to top of beg ch-3. Fasten and end off both yarns—80 sts.

Welt
With RS facing and C, join to any st, ch 1 and sc in each st around, join with sl st to first st.
Next rnd (WS) Ch 1 and turn, sc in each st around, join to beg, fasten and end off.

Zig zag
With RS facing and A, join to back lp of any st.
Rnd 1 Ch 4 (counts as a tr). Working into the back lp of each st, *dc in each of next 2 sts, hdc in each of next 2 sts, sc in next st, hdc in each of next 2 sts, dc in each of next 2 sts, tr in next st; rep from * around, omitting last tr, join with sl st to top of ch-4. **Rnd 2 (WS)** Ch 3 (counts as a dc) and turn. Working through both lps of each st, dc in same st as turning ch, *hdc in each of next 2 dc, sc in next hdc, pick up lp in next hdc, skip next sc, pick up another lp in next hdc, yo and draw through all 3 lps on hook for sc-double-dec, sc in next hdc, hdc in each of next 2 dc, work 3 dc all in next tr for dc-double-inc; rep from * around end with only 1 extra dc in same turning ch as first st, join with sl st to top of beg ch 3, fasten and end off A.
Rnd 3 With RS facing and E, working through

(Continued on page 141)

Sweet Dreams

A cuddly afghan bids a gentle "good night" to sleepy wee ones. Crocheted granny squares are worked separately, then sewn together and trimmed in lacy crochet edging. "Sweet Dreams" first appeared in the Winter '02/'03 issue of *Family Circle Easy Knitting* magazine.

MATERIALS

- *Grace* by Patons®, 1¾oz/50g balls, each approx 136yd/125m (cotton)
  - 3 balls in #60416 lt pink (MC)
  - 2 balls each in #60027 mint (A), #60451 mango (B) and #60603 apricot (D)
  - 1 ball in #60611 yellow (C)
- Size E/4 (3.5mm) crochet hook OR SIZE TO OBTAIN GAUGE

FINISHED MEASUREMENTS

- Approx 25" x 28"/63.5 x 71cm

GAUGE

One square to 3"/7.5cm using size E/4 (3.5mm) crochet hook.
TAKE TIME TO CHECK YOUR GAUGE.

STITCH GLOSSARY

CL (cluster st)

Work 3 dc in the same ch-sp or st as stated in the edging directions.

BASIC GRANNY SQUARE

Note See placement diagram for color order of the first 3 rnds.

With first color, ch 4. Join ch with a sl st forming a ring.

Rnd 1 (RS) Ch 5 (counts as 1 dc and ch 2), [dc in ring, ch 2] 7 times. Join rnd with a sl st in 3rd ch of ch-5. Fasten off. **Rnd 2** Join 2nd color with a sl st in any ch-2 sp. Ch 3 (always counts as 1 dc), work 2 dc in same sp, ch 2, [work 3 dc in next ch-2 sp, ch 2] 7 times. Join rnd with a sl st in 3rd ch of ch-3. Fasten off. **Rnd 3** Join 3rd color with a sl st in any ch-2 sp. Ch 3, work (2 dc, ch 1, 3 dc) in same sp, ch 1, [work (3 dc, ch 1, 3 dc) in next ch-2 sp, ch 1] 7 times. Join rnd with a sl st in 3rd ch of ch-3. Fasten off. **Rnd 4** Join MC with a sl st in any ch-1 sp. Ch 3, work (2 dc, ch 1, 3 dc) in same sp (first corner made), ch 1, *[sc in next ch-1 sp, ch 2] twice, sc in next ch-1 sp, ch 1, work (3 dc, ch 1, 3 dc) in next ch-1 sp, ch 1; rep from * around, end [sc in next ch-1 sp, ch 2] twice, sc in next ch-1 sp, ch 1. Join rnd with a sl st in 3rd ch of ch-3. Fasten off.

Make 56 squares foll placement diagram for colorways.

FINISHING

Sew squares tog foll placement diagram.

Edging

Note On rnd 1, you will not only be working into the 4 outer corner ch-1 sps of the corner squares to form new corners, but as you work across each side edge of the blanket, you will also be working into the inner corner ch-1 sps of squares at the joined seams.

Rnd 1 (RS) Join MC with a sl st in any outer corner ch-1 sp. Ch 5 (counts as 1 hdc and ch 3), hdc in same sp (first corner made), ** *hdc in next ch-1 sp, ch 2, [hdc in next ch-2 sp, ch 2] twice, hdc in next ch-1 sp, ch 2, hdc in opposite corner ch-1 sp of same square, ch 2, sk joined seam, hdc in corner ch-1 sp of next square, ch 2; rep from * to next outer corner ch-1 sp, work (hdc, ch 3, hdc) in sp; rep from ** around. Join rnd with a sl st in 2nd ch of ch-5. Fasten off. **Rnd 2** Join A with a sl st in any corner ch-3 sp. Ch 3 (counts as 1 dc), work 4 dc in same sp (first corner made), ch 2, ** *CL in next ch-2 sp, ch 2, sk next ch-2 sp; rep from * to next corner ch-3 sp, work 5 dc in sp, ch 2; rep from ** around. Join rnd with a sl st in 3rd ch of ch-3. Fasten off. **Rnd 3** Join C with a sl st in first dc of any 5-dc corner. Ch 3 (counts as 1 dc), work 2 dc in same st, ch 1, work 5dc in 3rd dc of same corner, ch 1, work CL in 5th dc of same corner, ch 2, ** *CL in 2nd dc of next CL, ch 2; rep from * to next 5-dc corner, work (CL in first dc of corner, ch 1, 5 dc in 3rd dc, ch 1, CL in 5th dc) ch 2; rep from ** around. Join rnd with a sl st in 3rd ch of ch-3. Fasten off. **Rnd 4** Join B with a sl st in first dc of any 5-dc corner. Ch 3 (counts as 1 dc), work 2 dc in same st, ch 1, work 3dc in 3rd dc of same corner, ch 1, work CL in 5th dc of same corner, ch 2, ** *CL in 2nd dc of next CL, ch 2; rep from * to next 5-dc corner, work (CL in first dc of corner, ch 1, CL in 3rd dc, ch 1, CL in 5th dc) ch 2; rep from ** around. Join rnd with a sl st in 3rd ch of ch-3. Fasten off. **Rnd 5** Join D with a sl st in 2nd dc of any corner CL. Ch 7 (counts as 1 dc and ch 4), sl st in 4th ch from hook (picot made), dc in same st, ch 2, *sc in next ch-sp, dc in 2nd dc of next cluster, ch 4, sl st in 4th ch from hook, dc in same st, ch 2; rep from * around. Join rnd with a sl st in 3rd ch of ch-7. Fasten off.

(See diagram on page 142)

Wooly Wonder

for intermediate crocheters

A colorful stocking cap, complete with a spirited tassel at the end, is sure to make winter seem warmer. Designed by Cleckheaton Design Studio, it's a great weekend project. "Wooly Wonder" first appeared in the Winter '99/'00 issue of *Family Circle Easy Knitting* magazine.

MATERIALS

- *Cleckheaton Country 8 ply* by Plymouth Yarns, $1^3/_4$oz/50g balls, each approx 105yd/96m (wool)
  2 balls in #1979 purple (MC)
  1 ball each in #1860 iris (A) and #1548 blue (B)
- Size F/5 (4mm) crochet hook OR SIZE TO OBTAIN GAUGE

SIZE
One size.

FINISHED MEASUREMENTS
- Head circumference 21"/53.5cm
- Length 20"/51cm

GAUGE
19 sts and 20 rnds to 4"/10cm over pat st, using a F/5 (4mm) crochet hook.

PATTERN STITCH
*4 rnds sc, 1 rnd dc; rep from * (5 rnds) for pat st.

STRIPE PATTERN
*3 rnds B, 2 rnds A, 3 rnds MC, 2 rnds B, 3 rnds A, 2 rnds MC; rep from * (15 rnds) for stripe pat.

HAT

Beg at top, with B, ch 4. Join with sl st to first ch to form ring. Work in pat st and stripe pat as foll:

Foundation rnd Cont with B, ch 1, work 5 sc in ring, join with sl st to first st at end of this and every rnd. **Rnd 1** Sc in each sc. **Rnd 2** Work 2 sc in each sc—10 sc. **Rnd 3** Sc in each sc. **Rnd 4** With A, ch 3 (counts as 1 dc), sk first sc, dc in each of next 9 sc—10 dc. **Rnd 5** Sc in first st, *2 sc in next st, sc in next st; rep from * to last st, 2 sc in last st—15 sc. **Rnds 6 and 7** With MC, sc in each sc. **Rnd 8** Sc in next 2 sc, *2 sc in next sc, sc in next 2 sc; rep from * to last sc, 2 sc in last sc—20 sc. **Rnd 9** With B, dc in each sc. **Rnd 10** Cont with B, sc in each dc. **Rnd 11** With A, sc in next 3 sc, *2 sc in next sc, sc in 3 sc; rep from * to last sc, 2 sc in last sc—25 sc. **Rnds 12 and 13** Cont with A, sc in each sc. **Rnd 14** With MC, dc in each sc around. **Rnd 15** Cont with MC, sc in next 4 dc, *2 sc in next dc, sc in next 4 dc; rep from * to last st, 2 sc in last dc—30 sc. Now, work 15-rnd stripe pat again from beg, cont pat st as established and inc 5 sts evenly spaced on every 4th rnd (whether it's an sc row or a dc row). The last inc row should be rnd 71—100 sc. After rnd 71 has been completed, work 12 rnds even in pat st and stripe pat, end with MC and 3 rnds sc. Fasten off.

FINISHING

Tassel
With MC, wind yarn 8 times around a piece of cardboard 4"/10cm long to make tassel. Attach to top of hat.

Pretty in Pink
for advanced crocheters

Kelly Overbey's granny-square pullover tops every girl's wish list. The stylish boatneck and cool cropped shape are tastefully trendy. "Pretty in Pink," first appeared in the Spring/Summer '01 issue of *Family Circle Easy Knitting* magazine.

MATERIALS
- *Microspun* by Lion Brand Yarn Co., 2½oz/70g balls, each approx 168yd/154m (acrylic)
  10 balls in #101 pink
- Size E/4 (3.5mm) crochet hook OR SIZE TO OBTAIN GAUGE

SIZES
Sized for Small/Medium.

FINISHED MEASUREMENTS
- Bust 42"/106.5cm
- Length 18"/45.5cm
- Upper arm 13½"/34cm

GAUGE
Square measures 3"/7.5cm using size E/4 (3.5mm) hook.
TAKE TIME TO CHECK YOUR GAUGE.

Notes
1 Unless otherwise noted, ch-3 at beg of rnd counts as 1 dc and ch-4 counts as 1 dc and ch 1. The ch-1 sp is referred to as sp.
2 Corner is worked as 3 dc, ch 1 and 3 dc in corner sp.

BASIC SQUARE
(make 1)
Note Only one square is made in this way. All other squares are joining squares. Beg at center with size E/4 (3.5mm) hook, ch 4, join with a sl st of first ch to form ring.
Rnd 1 Ch 4, [3 dc in ring, ch 1] 3 times, 2 dc in ring, join with a sl st to 3rd ch of beg ch. **Rnd 2** Ch 3, in same sp work 2 dc, ch 1 and 3 dc (for first corner), [ch 1, skip 3 dc, in next sp work 3 dc, ch 1 and 3 dc for corner] 3 times, ch 1, sl to top of ch-3.

Rnd 3 Ch 3, in same sp work 2 dc, ch 1 and 3 dc, [ch 1, skip 3 dc, 3 dc in next sp, ch 1, skip 3 dc, in next sp work corner] 3 times, ch 1, skip 3 dc, 3 dc in next sp, ch 1, join with sl st to top of ch-3.
Rnd 4 Ch 3, in same sp work 2 hdc, ch 1 and 3 hdc, [*ch 1, skip 3 dc, 3 hdc in next sp*; rep between *'s once, ch 1, skip 3 dc, in next sp work 3 hdc, ch 1 and 3 hdc for corner] 3 times, then rep between *'s twice, ch 1, join with sl st to top of ch-3. Fasten off.

JOINING SQUARE
Work as for basic square for rnds 1-3. **Joining rnd 4** (This square is joined to first square) Ch 3, in same sp work 2 hdc, ch 1 and 3 hdc, [*ch 1, skip 3 dc, 3 hdc in next sp *; rep between *'s once, ch 1, skip 3 dc, in next sp work 3 hdc, ch 1 and 3 hdc for corner] twice, ch 1, skip 3 dc, 3 hdc in next sp; rep between *'s once, ch 1, skip 3 dc, in next sp work 3 hdc, insert hook into corresponding corner of first square, draw up a lp, yo and through 2 lps (sc joining made to first square), 3 dc in same sp to complete corner, work sc joining in first square, [ch 1, skip 3 dc, 3 hdc in next sp; work sc joining in first square]; rep between *'s twice, ch 1, join with sl st to top of ch-3. One square is now joined to first square. Cont to join each new square in this way for pieces foll schematic and explanations that foll.

FRONT AND BACK
Make and join 42 squares for front and 42 squares for back foll schematic diagram.

SLEEVES
Note Sleeves are made with ½ squares and ¾ squares at seam edges for shaping. Joining is worked as for basic square joining foll schematic and instructions for sleeves.

1/2 SQUARE
Work basic square rnd. Cont to work in rows, turning and working back and forth on RS and WS as foll: **Row 2** Ch 3, 2 dc in same sp, [ch 1, skip 3 dc, in next sp work 3 dc, ch 1 and 3 dc for corner] twice, end ch 1, skip 3 dc, 3 dc in next sp, turn. **Row 3** Ch 4, skip 2 dc, [3 dc in next sp, ch 1, skip 3 dc, in next sp work corner, ch 1, skip 3 dc] twice, end 3 dc in next sp, ch 1, dc in top of beg ch, turn. **Row 4** Ch 3, 2 dc in sp, [*ch 1, skip 3 dc, 3 dc in next sp*, ch 1, skip 3 dc, in next sp work corner, rep between *'s once] twice, end ch 1, skip 3 dc, dc in final sp. Fasten. The straight edge without corner dc's is the side seam edge.

3/4 SQUARE (left seam edge)
Work basic square rnds 1-3.
Row 4 In first corner work 1 sc, ch 1, * [skip 3 dc, 3 dc in next sp] twice, skip 3 dc, in next sp work corner, ch 1*; rep between *'s once; rep

(Continued on page 142)

Fine Lines

Vibrant stripes wake up this snuggly cozy blanket. Rebecca Rosen's single-crochet design can be done in a flash and is a perfect project for beginning crocheters. "Fine Lines" first appeared in the Winter '02/'03 issue of *Family Circle Easy Knitting* magazine.

MATERIALS

■ *Fashion Knit* by TMA Yarns, 3oz/85g balls (acrylic)

Girls

6 balls in #394 English rose (A)

3 balls each in #405 purple (B), #216 lavender (C), #102 black (D), #247 turquoise (E), #211 orange (F) and #218 red (G)

Boys

6 balls in #137 blue (A)

3 balls each in #286 green (B), #404 denim (C), #205 brown (D), #403 lemon (E), #365 lime green (F) and #211 orange (G)

■ Size K/10.5 (7mm) crochet hook OR SIZE TO OBTAIN GAUGE

FINISHED MEASUREMENTS

■ 46" x 56"/117 x 142cm

GAUGE

6 sc, ch 1 and 13 rows to 4"/10cm over pattern st using size K/10.5 (7mm) crochet hook. TAKE TIME TO CHECK YOUR GAUGE.

PATTERN STITCH

Row 1 Sc in 3rd ch from hook, *ch 1, skip 1 ch, sc in next ch; rep from *, end sc in last ch. Ch 2 turn. **Row 2** *Sc in next ch-1 sp, ch 1; rep from *, end sc in top of t-ch. Ch 2, turn. Rep row 2 for pat st.

STRIPE PAT

(both afghans)

*1 row B, 4 rows C, 1 row D, 2 rows E, 2 rows F, 4 rows G, 2 rows D, 1 row F, 2 rows B, 3 rows A, 1 row D, 2 rows C, 1 row E, 2 rows A; rep from * (28 rows) for stripe pat.

AFGHAN

With A, ch 149. Work in pat st and stripe pat until piece measures 56"/142cm. Do not fasten off.

Border

With A, beg at a corner, work sc, ch 1 and sc in next st (first corner worked), *skip next sp, sc in next sp, ch 1; rep from * to next corner, work sc, ch 1 and sc in next corner; rep from * around entire afghan. Join with sl st to first st. Rep last row twice more. Fasten off.

Braids

Cut 24"/61cm lengths of each color. Attach them at each corner. Braid for 4½"/11.5cm. Tie a piece of yarn around end and let rem length hang.

Cradle Comfort

for beginner crocheters

Awash in dreamy pastels, Margarita Mejia's chevron-striped coverlet is a welcome addition to baby's room. Cuddly soft and simple to stitch, it makes a heartfelt shower gift. "Cradle Comfort" first appeared in the Winter '02/'03 issue of *Family Circle Easy Knitting* magazine.

MATERIALS

■ *Grace* by Patons®, 1³/₄oz/50g balls, each approx 136yd/125m (cotton)
  2 balls each in #60130 lt blue (A), #60611 yellow (B), #60230 mint (C) and #60027 green (D)
■ Size E/4 (3.5mm) crochet hook OR SIZE TO OBTAIN GAUGE

FINISHED MEASUREMENTS

■ Approx 23¹/₂" x 27"/59.5 x 68.5cm

GAUGE

35 sts and 18 rows to 5"/12.5cm over pat st using size E/4 (3.5mm) crochet hook.
TAKE TIME TO CHECK YOUR GAUGE.

Notes

1 When changing colors on a dc row, draw new color through last 2 lps on hook to complete last dc.
2 When changing colors on a sc row, draw new color through 2 lps on hook to complete last sc.

BLANKET

With A, ch 171.
Row 1 (WS) Dc in 4th ch from hook, dc in next 6 ch, *work 3 dc in next ch, dc in next 7 ch, sk next 2 ch, dc in next 7 ch; rep from * across, end work 3 dc in next ch, dc in last 7 ch. Ch 3, turn. Cont to work through back lps only. **Row 2** Sk first st, *dc in next 7 sts, work 3 dc in next st, dc in next 7 sts, sk next 2 sts; rep from *, end dc in next 7 sts, work 3 dc in next st, dc in next 6 sts, sk next st, dc in last st. Join B, ch 1, turn. **Rows 3-6** Sk first st, *sc in next 7 sts, work 3 sc in next st, sc in next 7 sts, sk next 2 sts; rep from * end sc in next 7 sts, work 3 sc in next st, sc in next 6 sts, sk next st, sc in last st. Ch 1, turn. After row 6 is completed, join C, ch 3, turn. **Rows 7 and 8** Rep row 2. After row 8 is completed, join D, ch 1, turn. **Rows 9-12** Rep row 3. After row 12 is completed, join A, ch 3, turn. **Rows 13 and 14** Rep row 2. After row 14 is completed, join B, ch 1, turn. Rep rows 3-14 for pat st and stripe pat. Work even until piece measures 27"/68.5cm from beg, end with row 14. Fasten off.

FINISHING

Block lightly.

Girl Power

for intermediate crocheters

A cheerful mosaic of large and small two-toned blossoms combine in this charming little cardigan. Made by joining flowers together with a simple slip stitch, the boxy style and dropped shoulders keep things ultra-simple. "Girl Power" first appeared in the Spring/Summer '03 issue of *Family Circle Easy Knitting*.

MATERIALS
- *Grace* by Patons®, 1³/₄oz/50g balls, each approx 136yd/125m (cotton)
  1 ball each in #603222 purple (A) and #60321 lilac (C)
  2 balls each in #60438 dk pink (B) and #60604 orange (D)
  3 balls in #60416 pink (E).
- One each sizes C/2 (2.75mm), D/3(3mm), E/4 (3.5mm) and F/5 (4mm) hooks
  OR SIZE TO OBTAIN GAUGE
- 3³/₄"/20mm buttons

SIZE
Sized for Girl's 6.

FINISHED MEASUREMENTS
- Chest 31"/78.5cm
- Length 14¹/₂"/37 cm
- Upper arm 9¹/₂"/24 cm

GAUGES
- Motif 1 measures 2¹/₂" x 2¹/₂"/6cm x 6cm square using size E/4 (3.5mm) hook.
- Motif 2 measures 1¹/₂" x 1¹/₂"/4cm x 4cm square using size C/2 (2.75mm)hook.
TAKE TIME TO CHECK YOUR GAUGES.

Motif 1
With A and designated hook size, ch8, join with sl st to first ch to form ring.
Rnd 1 Ch 1, work 16 sc into ring, drop A and join B with a sl st to first sc.
Rnd 2 Ch 3, work 1 dc in same sc as joining, *ch 4, 1 dc in each of next 2 sc; rep from *, end ch 4, join E with a sl st to top of ch-3—8 ch-4 loops.
Rnd 3 Ch 1, 1 sc each dc and 5 sc in each ch-4 loop around. Join to first sc and fasten off.

Motif 2
With C and designated hook size, ch 8, join with sl st to first ch to form ring.
Rnd 1 Ch 1, work 16 sc in ring, drop C and join D with a sl st to first sc.
Rnd 2 Ch 1, sl st in joining sc, *5 dc in next sc,

ch 1, sl st in next sc; rep from * 7 times more, end with sl st in sl st at beg of rnd. Fasten off.

BACK
Make 30 motif 1 flowers using size E/4 (3.5mm) hook. Make 28 motif 2 flowers using size C/2 (2.75mm) hook. Lay out as in diagram. Sl st tog with E at points as shown in photo.

LEFT FRONT
Make 14 motif 1 flowers using size E/4 (3.5mm) hook. Make 8 motif 2 flowers using size C/2 (2.75mm) hook. Lay out and join as in diagram.

RIGHT FRONT
Work motifs as for left front. Lay out with neck in reverse and join as before. Join fronts and back shoulders by folding over at motif 2 flowers from back. Join side seams by folding over back motif 2 flowers to join at fronts.

SLEEVES
Work 6 motif 1 flowers using size E/4(3.5mm) hook, 6 motif 1 flowers using size F/5(4mm) hook. (These 6 larger flowers will be at the top of the sleeve to make for a wider upper arm measurement). Work 6 motif 2 flowers using size C/2 (2.75mm) hook, 6 motif 2 flowers using size D/3 (3mm) hook. Join sleeves to armhole openings as other joinings.

FINISHING
Block to measurements.

Outer edging
Rnd 1 With size E/4(3.5mm) hook and E, work 1 sc in each sc around motif 1 flowers on edge with ch 5 between each motif. Join in first sc, ch 1.
Rnd 2 Work 1 sc in each sc and 5 sc in each ch-5 loop and work a ch-5 loop at the edge of the top 3 motif 1 flowers for each button loop on right front edge. Fasten off.

Sleeve edging
Work sleeve edging as for outer edging. Sew on buttons.

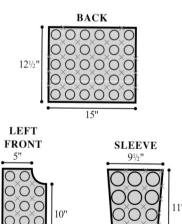

Crochet Basics

There's nothing quite as satisfying as creating something with your own two hands. In **Family Circle Easy Crochet**, our most inspiring and exciting projects from *Family Circle Easy Knitting* magazine have been compiled to form a comprehensive source of both classic and contemporary items that are sure to delight both novice and more experienced crocheters.

Whether giving a cozy, fun winter hat as a gift or making an indispensible summer tote for yourself, these portable crochet projects are perfect to take along everywhere you go. The results of your work will be a precious item that can be passed down through generations.

Use these patterns to experiment with different textures and colors in order to display your own unique style. Crocheting has never been so fun and easy!

SIZING

In order to ensure a perfect fit, it is important to measure the recipient to determine which size to make. Be sure there is enough ease in the finished measurements for a comfortable fit.

YARN SELECTION

For an exact reproduction of the projects photographed, use the yarn listed in the "Materials" section of the pattern. We've chosen yarns that are readily available in the U.S. and Canada at the time of printing. The Resources list on pages 143 provides addresses of yarn distributors. Contact them for the name of a retailer in your area.

YARN SUBSTITUTION

You may wish to substitute yarns. Perhaps you view small-scale projects as a chance to incorporate leftovers from your yarn stash, or the yarn specified may not be available in your area. You'll need to crochet to the given gauge to obtain the finished measurements with a substitute yarn. Be sure to consider how the fiber content of the substitute yarn will affect the comfort and the ease of care of your projects.

After you've successfully gauge-swatched a substitute yarn, you'll need to figure out how much of the substitute yarn the project requires. First, find the total length of the original yarn in the pattern (multiply number of balls by yards/meters per ball). Divide this figure by the new yards/meters per ball (listed on the ball band). Round up to the next whole number. The answer is the number of balls required.

GAUGE

It is important to crochet a gauge swatch to achieve the correct finished measurement of any project. The type of hook used—plastic, wood or metal—will influence gauge, so work your swatch with the hook you plan to use for the project. Make the swatch at least 4"/10cm square in the pattern stated in the gauge and using the suggested hook size. Launder and block your gauge swatch before taking measurements. Measure the swatch over the entire width and length. Try different hook sizes until your sample measures the required number of stitches and rows. To get fewer stitches to the inch/cm, use a larger hook; to get more stitches to the inch/cm, use a smaller hook. It's a good idea to keep your gauge swatch to test any embroidery or embellishment, as well as blocking, and cleaning methods.

FOLLOWING CHARTS/DIAGRAMS

Charts are a convenient way to follow colorwork, openwork, cable, and other stitch patterns at a glance. When crocheting back and forth in rows, unless otherwise indicated, read charts from right to left on right side (RS) rows and from left to right on wrong side (WS) rows, repeating any stitch and row repeats as directed in the pattern. On some charts, the row numbers show you how to read the chart. For example, if row 1 is on the left-hand side of the chart, read that row from left to right, and if the subsequent row 2 is on the right-hand side of the chart, read row 2 from right to left. Posting a self-adhesive note under your working row is an easy way to keep track of your place on a chart.

Many patterns use placement diagrams to show how to join together individual motifs. This visual method is much easier to follow than a written explanation.

COLORWORK

Two main types of colorwork are explored in this book.

STRANDING

When motifs are closely placed, colorwork is

SKILL LEVELS

BEGINNER
Ideal first project.

EASY
Basic stitches, minimal shaping, simple finishing.

INTERMEDIATE
Patterns with complicated shaping and finishing.

ADVANCED
Challenging patterns; shaping and finishing require expert skills.

accomplished by stranding along two or more colors per row. While crocheting, hold the unworked color to the back of the work, securing it into each stitch by crocheting over the loose strand.

In some instances, such as when using highly contrasting colors like black and white, the unworked color may show through to the front of the work. In this case, do not crochet over the unused color, but rather "float" the strand at the back of the work. While crocheting, be sure to carry the unworked color slightly looser than the length of the float at the back to keep the work from puckering. As a general rule, do not carry unworked yarn for more than three stitches without securing it in the back. When making your guage swatch, practice with both methods to see which will work better for your project.

INTARSIA

Intarsia is accomplished with separate bobbins of individual colors. This method is ideal for large blocks of color or for motifs that aren't repeated close together. When changing colors, always leave the last two loops on the hook at the stitch before the color change, then draw the new color through. Continue with this new color for the number of stitches indicated in the pattern chart. You can also carry the colors not in use along the back as in stranding, to avoid weaving in the strands after the piece is completed.

BLOCKING

Blocking is an all-important finishing step in the crochet process. It is the best way to shape pattern pieces and smooth crocheted edges in preparation for sewing together. Most garments retain their shape if the blocking stages in the instructions are followed carefully. Choose a blocking method according to the yarn care label and when in doubt, test-block your gauge swatch.

WET BLOCK METHOD

Using rust-proof pins, affix pieces to measurements on a flat surface and lightly dampen using a spray bottle. Allow to dry before removing pins.

STEAM BLOCK METHOD

With WS facing, pin pieces. Steam lightly,

LAZY DAISY STITCH

holding the iron 2"/5cm above the knitting. Do not press or it will flatten stitches.

FINISHING

In crochet, projects are constructed in various ways. Items such as "Worth Repeating" on page 8 use the more traditional method of creating separate pieces and joining them together, which can be done either by sewing with a yarn needle or crocheting with a slip stitch.

"Cape Crusader" on page 36 eliminates the need for seaming by working the garment in the round. When using this method, it is helpful to place a stitch marker at the beginning of each round to help you keep your place.

Yet another form of construction appears in the pattern for "Bare Essential" on page 60, where medallion are made separately, then joined with a slip stitch. Similarly, in "Tote-a-Tote" on page 76, several identical motifs are crocheted and then sewn together.

CARE

Refer to the yarn label for the recommended cleaning method. Many of the projects in the book can be either washed by hand, or in the machine on a gentle or wool cycle, in lukewarm water with a mild detergent. Do not agitate, or soak for more than 10 minutes. Rinse gently with tepid water, then fold in a towel and gently press the water out. Lay flat to dry away from excess heat and light. Check the yarn band for any specific care instructions such as dry cleaning or tumble drying.

FRINGE

Cut yarn twice desired length plus extra for knotting. On wrong side, insert hook from front to back through piece and over folded yarn. Pull yarn through. Draw ends through and tighten. Trim yarn.

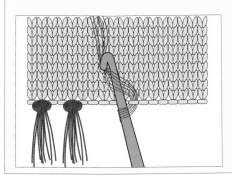

TASSELS

Cut a piece of cardboard to the desired length of the tassel. Wrap yarn around the cardboard. Knot a piece of yarn tightly around one end, cut as shown, and remove the cardboard. Wrap and tie yarn around the tassel about 1"/2.5cm down from the top to secure the fringe.

CROCHET STITCHES

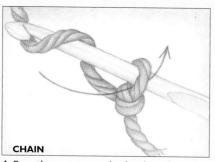

CHAIN

1 Pass the yarn over the hook and catch it with the hook.

2 Draw the yarn through the loop on the hook.

3 Repeat steps 1 and 2 to make a chain.

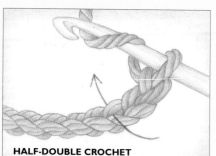

SINGLE CROCHET

1 Insert the hook through top two loops of a stitch. Pass the yarn over the hook and draw up a loop—two loops on hook.

2 Pass the yarn over the hook and draw through both loops on hook.

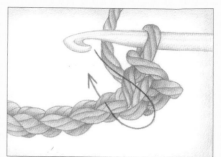

3 Continue in the same way, inserting the hook into each stitch.

HALF-DOUBLE CROCHET

1 Pass the yarn over the hook. Insert the hook through the top two loops of a stitch.

2 Pass the yarn over the hook and draw up a loop—three loops on hook. Pass the yarn over the hook.

3 Draw through all three loops on hook.

DOUBLE CROCHET

1 Pass the yarn over the hook. Insert the hook through the top two loops of a stitch.

2 Pass the yarn over the hook and draw up a loop—three loops on hook.

3 Pass the yarn over the hook and draw it through the first two loops on the hook, then pass the yarn over the hook and draw through the remaining two loops. Continue in the same way, inserting the hook into each stitch.

Illustrations: Joni Coniglio

Try crochet for a new spin on an old favorite. Here, "cables" are worked in front post double crochet stitches on every right-side row. The "bobbles" are a cluster of unfinished double crochet stitches, worked together to form balls.

To work the basic three-stitch cable, you need a base of three front post double crochet stitches. To work a front post stitch, yarn over and insert the hook from front to back to front around the post of the next stitch, but one row below, as shown. Then complete the double crochet.

To work the left twist, skip the first post stitch, work the next two post stitches, then go back to the first post stitch and complete the front post double crochet, as shown.

Making a center post stitch, work a post stitch to the right of the center stitch on the next right-side row as follows: Work to one stitch before the center post stitch, work a front post stitch around the center stitch to form a right twist, as shown. Complete the right twist by working a single crochet in the skipped stitch.

To work the left twist, skip the next stitch, then work a single crochet in the following stitch, then work a front post stitch around the center post stitch, as shown. Always work a post stitch around the previous post stitch.

*Yarn over hook, insert hook into next stitch, yarn over and draw loop through, yarn over and through two loops on hook; rep from * twice more, inserting hook into same stitch. There are four loops on hook as shown.

Yarn over and draw through three loops. To complete bobble, yarn over and draw through last two loops, as shown.

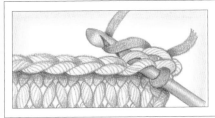

SLIP STITCH
Insert the crochet hook into a stitch, catch the yarn and pull up a loop. Draw the loop through the loop on the hook.

Crochet Terms and Abbreviations

approx approximately

beg begin(ning)

CC contrast color

ch chain(s)

cm centimeter(s)

cont continu(e)(ing)

dc double crochet (UK: tr–treble)

dec decrease(ing)–[yo, draw up lp in next st, yo adn through 2lps] twice, yo and through all 3 lps on hook.

dpn double-pointed needle(s)

dtr double treble (UK: trtr—triple treble)

foll follow(s)(ing)

g gram(s)

garter stitch Knit every row. Circular knitting: knit one round, then purl one round.

grp(s) group(s)

hdc half double crochet (UK: htr–half treble)

inc increase(ing)–Work two stitches into the same stitch.

LH left-hand

lp(s) loop(s)

m meter(s)

MC main color

mm millimeter(s)

no stitch On some charts, "no stitch" is indicated with shaded spaces where stitches have been decreased or not yet made. In such cases, work the stitches of the chart, skipping over the "no stitch" spaces.

oz ounce(s)

pat(s) pattern

pm place markers–Place or attach a loop of contrast yarn or purchased stitch marker as indicated.

rem remain(s)(ing)

reverse sc work single crochet from left to right.

rep repeat

rnd(s) round(s)

RH right-hand

RS right side(s)

sc single crochet (UK: dc–double crochet)

sk skip

sl st slip stitch (UK: sc–single crochet)

sp(s) space(s)

st(s) stitch(es)

tbl through back of loop

t-ch turning chain

tog together

tr treble (UK: dtr—double treble)

trtr triple treble (UK: qtr—quadruple treble)

WS wrong side(s)

work even Continue in pattern without increasing or decreasing. (UK: work straight)

yd yard(s)

yo yarn over

* = Repeat directions following * as many times as indicated.

[ ] = Repeat directions inside brackets as many times as indicated.

CROCHET HOOKS	
US	**METRIC**
14 steel	.60mm
12 steel	.75mm
10 steel	1.00mm
6 steel	1.50mm
5 steel	1.75mm
B/1	2.00mm
C/2	2.50mm
D/3	3.00mm
E/4	3.50mm
F/5	4.00mm
G/6	4.50mm
H/8	5.00mm
I/9	5.50mm
J/10	6.00mm
	6.50mm
K/10½	7.00mm

LACED WITH GRACE

(Continued from page 12)

Row 3 Work pat row 3, end with 1 sc, ch 5, 1 sc, ch 2 and 1 dc in last dc. **Row 4** Ch 3, 1 dc in ch-2 sp, ch 3, work flower in next dc, ch 3, dc in center sp of next flower, end ch 3, 1 sc, ch 5, 1 sc, ch 2 and 1 dc in 3rd ch of t-ch. **Row 5** Work 3 (3, 5, 5) ch-4 sps. Work until same length as back. Fasten off 15 (15, 25, 25) dc.

RIGHT FRONT

Work same as left front (pattern is reversible).

SLEEVES

With chosen hook size, ch 32 (32, 42, 42). Work in pat st on 30 (30, 40, 40) dc through row 5. **(Inc) Row 6** Ch 3, 1 dc in first st (inc), 4 dc (instead of 3 dc) in first ch-4 sp (inc), work pat to last st, 2 dc in last st (inc)—33 (33, 43, 43) dc. **(Inc) Row 2** Inc 1 st at beg and end of row—35 (35, 45, 45) dc. **Row 3** Ch 5, skip 2 dc, 1 dc in next dc, ch 3, rep from * of pat row 3, end ch 3, skip 1 dc, 1 dc in top of t-ch. **Row 4** Ch 3, skip ch-3 sp, [1 sc, ch 5] twice, and 1 sc in next dc, rep from * of pat row 4, end ch 2, 1 dc in 3rd ch of ch-5. **Row 5** Ch 1, sc in ch 2-sp, ch 2, 1 sc in center of flower, rep from * of pat row 5, end ch 2, 1 sc in last ch-3 sp. **Row 6** Ch 3, work pat row 6, working 3 dc in first ch-2 sp and 4 dc in last ch-2 sp—40 (40, 50, 50) dc. Cont to inc in this way, every row 6 and row 2, until there are 60 (60, 70, 70) dc. Work even until piece measures 16"/40.5cm from beg, end pat row 5.

Cap shaping

Work between *'s rows 6 (2, 3, 4, 5) of back armhole. Then work 40 (40, 50, 50) sc, instead of dc in each sp as on row 6. Fasten off.

FINISHING

Block pieces lightly to measurements. Sew shoulder seams (through back lps only). Sew sleeves into armholes. Sew side and sleeve seams.

Cuffs

Work 2 rnds sc around cuff. **Next rnd** Ch 1, *skip 2 sc, 5 dc in next sc (shell), skip 2 sc, sc in next sc; rep from * end skip 2 sc, 5 dc in next sc, skip 2 sc, sc in last sc. Join.

Front edge

Row 1 Join at right front corner and work 4 sc in each dc section, 5 sc in each lace section to top edge, 24 sc around front neck, 30 sc in back lps only of back neck, 24 sc around front neck, sc along left front as before to lower edge. Ch 1, turn. **Row 2** Work 1 sc in each sc, 3 sc in corners and dec 1 sc at each shoulder joining. Ch 1, turn. **Row 3** 1 sc in first 2 sc, *ch 1, skip 1 sc (buttonhole), sc in next 8 sc; rep from * 8 times, end last rep sc in last 7 sc, ch 2 at corner, do not skip 1 sc, sc around neck (with 1 dec at each shoulder) and down left front, then cont to work 1 sc in each dc at lower edge. Do not turn. **Rnd 4** Work 1 sc in each sc along front edge including buttonholes, 3 sc in ch-2 lp at corner, work shell edge around neck, sc along left front, shell edge along entire lower edge. Join and fasten off. Sew on buttons.

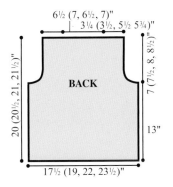

BACK
6½ (7, 6½, 7)"
3¼ (3½, 5½ 5¾)"
20 (20½, 21, 21½)"
7 (7½, 8, 8½)"
13"
17½ (19, 22, 23½)"

LEFT FRONT
3¼ (3½, 5½, 5¾)"
7 (7½, 8, 8½)"
17½"
13'
8¾ (9½, 11, 11¾)"

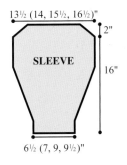

SLEEVE
13½ (14, 15½, 16½)"
2"
16"
6½ (7, 9, 9½)"

ARAN ARTISTRY

(Continued from page 18)

Neckband

With RS facing, work 72 (72, 78) sc evenly around neck edge, including top of sleeves. Join and work in rnds as foll: **Rnd 1** Sc in each st. **Rnd 2** *Sc in next 3 sts, fpdc in next 3 sts; rep from * around. Rep last 2 rnds once more, then work rnd 1 once more. On next rnd, work 3-st LT over post sts. Work 4 rnds even. Fasten off.

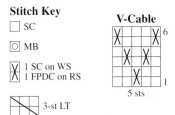

Stitch Key
☐ SC
◉ MB
Ⅴ 1 SC on WS
1 FPDC on RS
⬚ 3-st LT

V-Cable
6
1
5 sts

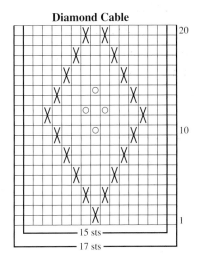

Diamond Cable
20
10
1
15 sts
17 sts

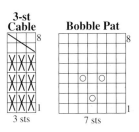

3-st Cable
8
1
3 sts

Bobble Pat
8
1
7 sts

(Continued on page 130)

(Continued from page 129)

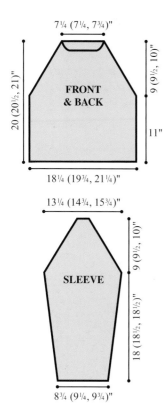

7¼ (7¼, 7¾)"

FRONT & BACK

20 (20½, 21)"

9 (9½, 10)"

11"

18¼ (19¾, 21¼)"

13¼ (14¾, 15¾)"

SLEEVE

9 (9½, 10)"

18 (18½, 18½)"

8¾ (9¼, 9¾)"

CORPORATE CLASSIC

(Continued from page 26)

Cap shaping

Leave off 3 (4, 5, 6) sts at each side of next row. Then leave off 2 sts at each side of next 14 rows, 1 st at each side of next 0 (0, 0, 1) row. Fasten off last 11 (14, 16, 17) sts.

FINISHING

Block pieces to measurements. Sew shoulder seams. Sew sleeves into armholes. Sew side and sleeve seams. Place markers for 6 buttons along right front, the first one at 1"/2.5cm from lower edge, the last one at ½"/1cm from neck edge and the others evenly spaced between. Work 5 rnds of sc all around neck, fronts and lower edges, working 3 sc in each corner and working a buttonhole in left front opposite markers by ch 2 and skip 2 sc on 3rd rnd. On next rnd, work 2 sc into ch-2 sp. After 5 rnds are completed, working from left to right, work 1 reverse sc in each sc. Fasten off.

Pocket flaps

(make 2)

Ch 21, work in sc for 6 rows on 20 sts. Then ch 1, and work 1 reverse sc along sides and lower edge of flap. Make 2 more flaps over 17 sc. Sew flaps to jacket as shown. Sew on buttons.

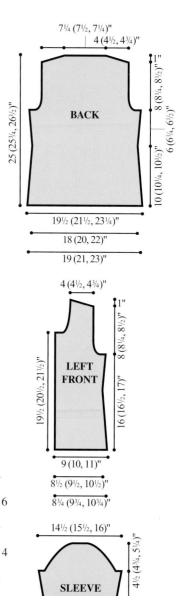

7¼ (7½, 7¼)"
4 (4½, 4¾)"

BACK

1"

8 (8¼, 8½)"

6 (6¼, 6½)"

25 (25¾, 26½)"

10 (10¼, 10½)"

19½ (21½, 23¼)"

18 (20, 22)"

19 (21, 23)"

4 (4½, 4¾)"

1"

LEFT FRONT

8 (8¼, 8½)"

19½ (20½, 21½)"

16 (16½, 17)"

9 (10, 11)"

8½ (9½, 10½)"

8¾ (9¾, 10¾)"

14½ (15½, 16)"

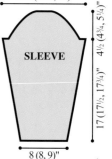

SLEEVE

4½ (4¾, 5¼)"

17 (17½, 17¾)"

8 (8, 9)"

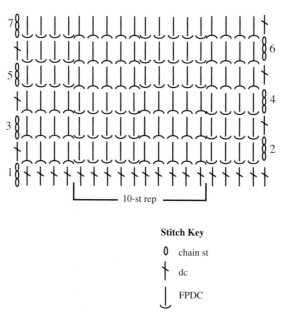

7

8

5

6

3

4

1

2

10-st rep

Stitch Key

0   chain st

†   dc

⌐   FPDC

⌐   BPDC

(Continued from page 34)

CHART 1

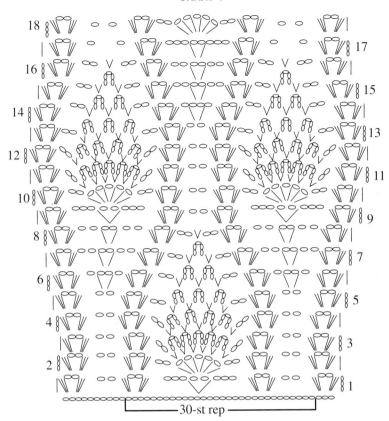

30-st rep

CHART 2

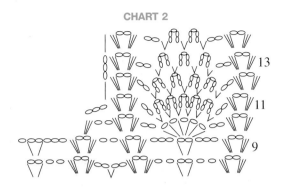

Stitch Key

○ Chain

∨ sc

| dc

〳〵 Cluster:
3dc, ch2, 3dc

MESH-MERIZING

(Continued from page 48)

Next row Sc in each st and each sp dec 0 (10) sts evenly—47 (81) sts. Ch 1, turn. Work 1 sc in each sc. Fasten off.

FINISHING

Block piece to measurements. Sew shoulder seams for 6½ (10½)"/16.5 (26.5)cm. Place markers at 6¾ (10¾)"/17 (27.5)cm down from shoulders. Sew sleeves to armholes between markers. Sew sleeve seams. Leaving 4"/10cm open at lower edge, sew side seams. Work 1 rnd of sc around neck edge. Ch 1. Work 1 rnd of sc in back lp of each sc around. Work lower edge trim and side slit trim in same way.

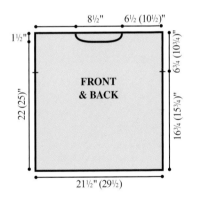

FRONT & BACK

8½"   6½ (10½)"
1½"
22 (25)"
6¾ (10¾)"
16¾ (15¾)"
21½ (29½)"

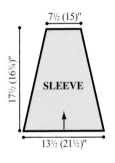

SLEEVE

7½ (15)"
17½ (16¾)"
13½ (21½)"

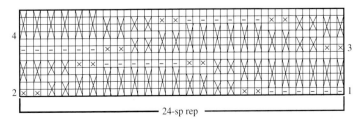

4   3

2   1

24-sp rep

Stitch Key

☐ ch-1 sp   ⊠ sc   〵 dc   ⤬ tr   〤 dtr

⊟ sl st

SHORT TAKE

(Continued from page 54)

t-ch sp, dc in 3rd ch of t-ch, turn. **Row 12** Ch 3, (2 dc, ch 2, 3 dc) in first v-st, ch 3, pat to last v-st, (3 dc, ch 2, 2 dc) in last v-st, dc in top of t-ch, turn. **Row 13** Ch 5, v-st in first shell, pat to last shell, v-st in last shell, ch 2, dc in top of t-ch, turn. **Row 14** Ch 4, work shell in first v-st, pat to last v-st, work shell in last v-st, ch 1, dc in 3rd ch of t-ch, turn. **Rows 15 and 16** Rep rows 13 and 14. **Row 17** Ch 7, v-st in first shell, pat to last shell, v-st in last shell, ch 4, dc in 2nd ch of t-ch, turn. **Row 18** Ch 6, work shell in first v-st, pat to last v-st, work shell in last v-st, ch 3, dc in 5th ch of t-ch, turn. **Row 19** Ch 5, dc in first dc, ch 4, v-st in first shell, pat to last shell, v-st in last shell, ch 4, (dc, ch 2, dc) in 4th ch of t-ch, turn. **Row 20** Ch 5, dc in first ch-2 sp, ch 3, work shell in next v-st, pat to last complete v-st, work shell in this v-st, ch 3, dc in t-ch sp, ch 2, dc in 3rd ch of t-ch, turn. **Row 21** Ch 5, dc in first ch-2 sp, ch 4, v-st in next shell, pat to last shell, v-st in last shell, ch 4, dc in t-ch sp, ch 2, dc in 3rd ch of t-ch, turn. **Row 22** Rep row 20. **Row 23** Ch 3, v-st in first ch-2 sp, pat to t-ch sp, v-st in t-ch sp, dc in 3rd ch of t-ch, turn. **Row 24** Ch 3, v-st in first v-st, pat to last v-st, v-st in last v-st, dc in top of t-ch, turn. Rep rows 1 to 14 (10) again, then work 5 (9) rows even as established in lace pat. Place a yarn marker at each end of last row, then work 6 rows even in lace pat as established. Fasten off.

FINISHING

Block pieces very lightly.

Back lower border

With RS facing, rejoin yarn in base of first ch at lower edge of back, ch 1, then work 1 sc in base of each ch to end—99 (123) sc.
Row 1 Ch 3, v-st in 2nd sc, *skip 2 sc, v-st in next sc; rep from * to last sc, dc in last sc, turn.
Row 2 *Ch 3, sc in sp between next 2 v-sts; rep from * ending ch 3, sc in top of t-ch, turn. **Row 3** Ch 1, *4 sc in next ch-3 sp; rep from * ending sl st in first ch of row 2. Fasten off.

Front lower borders

With RS facing, rejoin yarn in base of first ch at lower edge of each front, ch 1, then work 1 sc in base of each ch to end—51 (63) sc.

Complete as for back lower border.

Sleeve lower borders

With RS facing, rejoin yarn in base of first ch at lower edge of sleeve, ch 1, then work 1 sc in base of each ch to end—51 (63) sc. Complete as for back lower border.

Front and neck border

With RS facing, rejoin yarn at lower inner edge of right front border, ch 1 and sc evenly up right front, across back neck and down left front, working a multiple of 3 sc. Complete as for back lower border. Using ch-2 sp of v-st on border for buttonholes, mark position of 5 buttonholes on right front border, with the first one in 2nd v-st, the last one at 1"/2.5cm below neck shaping and the others spaced evenly between. Sew on buttons opposite buttonholes.

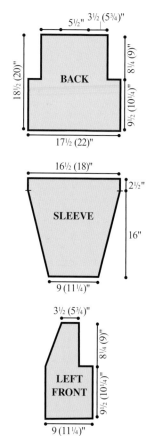

VEST DRESSED

(Continued from page 58)

Front edge and lower edge

Working around lower, front and neck edges, work as for Rnds 1 and 2 of armhole bands (working 3 sc in lower corners). Place markers for 6 buttonholes evenly spaced along right front. **Rnd 3** Ch 3, *dc in each sc to marker, ch 1, sk 1 sc; rep from * 5 times more, then cont dc around. On next rnd, work sc in each ch-1 sp. Finish as for armhole bands. Sew on buttons.

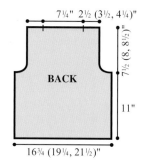

SWEET TREAT

(Continued from page 38)

RIGHT FRONT

Work to correspond to left front, reversing all shaping.

SLEEVES

Ch 55 (57, 59, 61). Work in pat st on 53 (55, 57, 59) sts as for back for 5 rows. **Row 6 (WS):** Dec row Ch 1, skip first st, 1 sc in each of next 25 (26, 27, 28) sts, skip center st, sc to last 2 sts, skip next st, sc in top of t-ch. Work 7 rows even. **Row 14** Rep row 6. Work 7 rows even. **Row 22** Rep row 6—44 (46, 48, 50) sts. Work even through row 50 (50, 52, 52). Piece measures approx 18 (18, 19, 19)"/45.5 (45.5, 48, 48)cm.

Cap shaping

Row 1 (RS) Do not ch, sl st in first 4 (5, 4, 5) sts, hdc in next st, dc to last 5 (6, 5, 6) sts, hdc in next st, leave rem 4 (5, 4, 5) sts unworked. **Row 2** Dec 1 sc at each end of row. **Row 3** Dec 1 dc at each end of row. Rep last 2 rows 5 (5, 6, 6) times more—12 sts. Fasten off.

FINISHING

Block pieces to measurements. Sew shoulder seams. Working from RS, work 1 row sc around fronts and back neck. Ch 1, turn. Place markers for 5 buttonholes along right front edge, the first one at beg of neck shaping, the last one at 3 sc from lower edge and the others evenly spaced between. **Next row (WS)** Working in sc, *sc to marker, ch 2 and skip 2 sc (buttonhole); rep from * 4 times more, end sc in last 3 sc. Ch 1, turn. **Next row** Working in sc, work 2 sc in each ch-2 lp. Ch 1, do not turn. **Next row (RS)** Working in reverse (from left to right), work 1 reverse sc in each sc around. Fasten off. Sew sleeves into armholes. Sew side and sleeve seams. Sew on

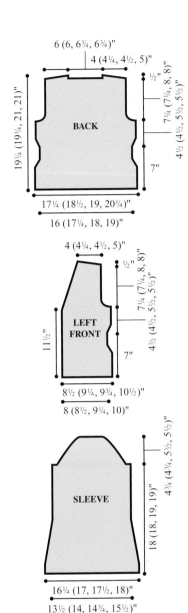

THINK TANK

(Continued from page 46)

forming corded edge. Work edge in same way around other armhole, lower and neck edges.

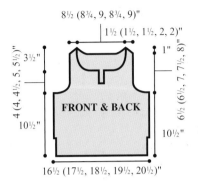

SHEER DELIGHT

(Continued from page 50)

sc in back ch around. Join with sl st. **Rnd 2** *Ch 4, skip 1 sc, sl st in next sc; rep from * around. Join and fasten off. Work edge in same way around armhole and neck edges.

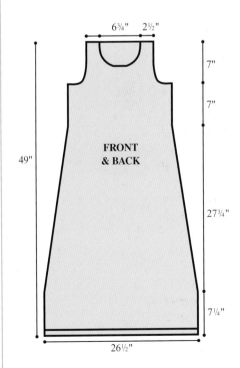

IN BLOOM

(Continued from page 52)

work even until piece measures approx 2 (2, 2½, 3)"/5 (5, 6, 7.5)cm from beg. Ch 3, turn. **Next (inc) row** V-st in first st, *sk next dc and ch-1, V-st in next st; rep from *, end V-st in last st, dc in 3rd ch of t-ch. Ch 3, turn. **Next row** Dc in first st, *sk next dc and ch-1, V-st in next st; rep from *, end dc in 3rd ch of t-ch. Ch 3, turn. Work even for 3 (3, 3, 2) rows. Rep these 4 (4, 4, 3) rows 7 (8, 8, 9) times more—34 (36, 38, 40) V-sts. Work even until piece measures 18 (18½, 19, 19)"/45.5 (47, 48, 48)cm from beg. Fasten off.

SPIDER FLOWER

(make 3)

With smaller hook, ch 4. Join ch with a sl st forming a ring. **Rnd 1 (RS)** Ch 1, work 8 sc in ch. Join rnd with a sl st in ch-1. **Rnd 2** Ch 1, *sc in next st, work 2 sc in next st; rep from * around—12 sts. Join rnd with a sl st in ch-1. **Rnd 3** Rep rnd 2—18 sts. Join rnd with a sl st in ch-1. **Rnd 4 (petals)** *Ch 9, sc in 2nd ch from hook and in next 7 ch, sl st in front lp of next st of rnd 3; rep from * around—18 petals. Turn to WS. *Ch 9, sc in 2nd ch from hook and in next 7 ch, sl st in back lp of next st of rnd 3; rep from * around—18 petals. Fasten off.

CARNATION

(make 3)

With smaller hook, ch 4. Join ch with a sl st forming a ring. **Rnd 1** Ch 1, work 8 sc in ch. Join rnd with a sl st in ch-1. **Rnd 2** Ch 1, *sc in next st, work 2 sc in next st; rep from * around—12

sts. Join rnd with a sl st in ch-1. **Rnd 3** Rep rnd 2—18 sts. Join rnd with a sl st in ch-1. **Rnd 4** Rep rnd 2—27 sts. Join rnd with a sl st in ch-1. **Rnd 5** Ch 1, *sc in next 2 sts, work 2 sc in next st; rep from * around—36 sts. Join rnd with a sl st in ch-1. **Rnd 6 (petals)** *Ch 7, dc in 3rd ch from hook and in next 4 ch, sl st in next st of rnd 5; rep from * around—36 petals. Join rnd with a sl st in first ch of ch-9. Fasten off.

DAISY

(make 10)

With smaller hook, ch 7, dc in 3rd ch from hook, dc in next 3 ch, work (dc, sc) in last ch, [ch 7, dc in 3rd ch from hook, dc in next 4 ch, sc in sc of first petal] 6 times. Fasten off.

FINISHING

Block pieces to measurements. Sew shoulder seams.

Neck edging

With RS facing and larger hook, join yarn with a sl st in left shoulder seam. **Rnd 1** Ch 1, work 163 sc evenly around entire neck edge. Join rnd with a sl st in ch-1. **Rnd 2** Ch 1, *sc in next 14 sts, dec 1 st over next 2 sts, rep from * around—153 sts. **Rnd 3** Ch 3, dc in each st around. Join rnd with a sl st in 3rd ch of ch-3. **Rnd 4** Ch 1, *sc in next 15 sts, dec 1 st over next 2 sts, rep from * around—144 sts. Join rnd with a sl st in ch-1. **Rnd 5** Rep rnd 3. **Rnd 6** Ch 1, sc in each st around. Join rnd with a sl st in ch-1. Fasten off. Place markers 9 (9½, 10, 10½)"/23 (24, 25,5, 26.5)cm down from shoulder seams

on front and back. Sew sleeves between markers. Sew side and sleeve seams. Referring to photo, sew one spider flower to right neck, one to upper left front and one to upper left sleeve. Sew one carnation to lower left front and one to center of each sleeve, right above cuff. Sew seven daisies onto front, as shown, and three on back as desired.

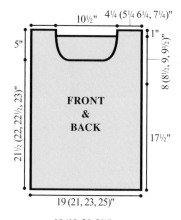

SOFT FOCUS

(Continued from page 56)

yarn, from RS rejoin 2 strands of yarn and sl st in each hdc across waistband of skirt, 3 sc in corner, then working into edge st only, work 30 sc along back side seam to 7"/18cm from top edge, ch 1, turn. Sc in each sc along placket edge. Fasten off. Sl st rem of side seam closed from WS. Sew on snaps to WS of the front

placket and to the RS of the back placket. Snap closed at placket edge.

Scalloped Edge

Beg at side seam edge, * in ch-9 lp work 1 sc, 8 hdc, 1 sc, skip 1 sc, sl st in next sc, skip next sc; rep from * around lower edge of skirt. Fasten off.

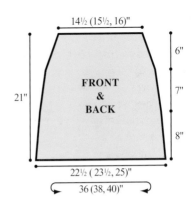

BARE ESSENTIAL

(Continued from page 60)

LARGE TOP

Half motif

(make 4)

Ch 6 (counts as first dtr and one foundation ch). **Row 1 (WS)** Work 10 dtr in 5th ch (foundation ch) from hook. Ch 18 (counts as 1 dtr and ch 13), turn. **Row 2** Sk first st, [2 dtr in next st, dtr in next st, ch 7, 2 dtr in next st, dtr in next st, ch 13] twice, end dtr in last st. Fasten off. Set aside.

Motif A

(make 1)

Ch 6 (counts as first dtr and one foundation ch). **Rnd 1 (RS)** Work 16 dtr in 5th ch (foundation ch) from hook. Join rnd with a sl st in 5th ch of first dtr. **Rnd 2** Ch 5 (counts as 1 dtr), dtr in same ch as sl st, [dtr in next st, ch 13, 2 dtr in next st, dtr in next st, ch 7, 2 dtr in next st] 3 times, end dtr in next st, ch 13, 2 dtr in next st, dtr in next st, ch 7. Join rnd with a sl st in 5th ch of ch-5. Fasten off.

Motif B

(make 101)

Work as for motif A to rnd 2. **Rnd 2 (joining)** Ch 5 (counts as 1 dtr), dtr in same ch as sl st, dtr in next st, ch 6, sl st in ch-13 lp of motif A, ch 6, 2 dtr in next st, dtr in next st, ch 3, sl in ch-7 lp of motif A, ch 3, 2 dtr in next st, ch 6, sl in ch-13 lp of motif A, ch 6, [2 dtr in next st, dtr in next

st, ch 7, 2 dtr in next st, dtr in next st, ch 13] twice, end 2 dtr in next st, dtr in next st, ch 7. Join rnd with a sl st in 5th ch of ch-5. Fasten off. Cont to join motifs following placement diagram. At adjacent ch-13 lps, join motifs with ch 6, sl st in ch-13, ch 6. To prevent bulk at ch-13 joinings, sl st into the previous sl st. At adjacent ch-7 lps, join motifs with ch 3, sl st in ch-7, ch 3. Join half motifs at front neck edge in the same manner.

FINISHING

Lightly block piece to measurements.

Bottom edging

From RS, join yarn with a sl st in center ch of left side. **Rnd 1** Ch 1, sc in each ch and st around. Join rnd with a sl st in ch-1. **Rnd 2** Ch 1, sc in joining sl st, ch 4, sk next 4 sts, *sc in next st, ch 4, sk next 4 sts; rep from * around. Join rnd with a sl st in first sc. **Rnd 3** *Sk next 4 sts, work 7 tr in next st, sk next 4 sts, sl st in next st; rep from * around. Join rnd with a sl st. Fasten off.

Neck edging

From RS, join yarn with a sl st in center ch of front neck edge. Rep rnds 1-3 of bottom edging.

Armhole edging

From RS, join yarn with a sl st in right corner ch of armhole. Rep rnds 1-3 of bottom edging.

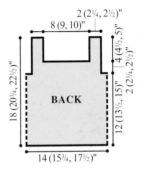

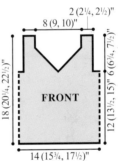

PLACEMENT DIAGRAM

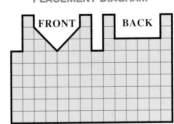

SUMMER SHOPPERS

(Continued from page 74)

1"/2.5cm at top and tack to inside of bag. Sew snap inside to center for closing.

KNAPSACK

Bottom circle

With larger hook, beg at center, ch 8, join with sl st to first ch to form ring. **Rnd 1** Ch 2 (does not count as 1 dc) work 19 dc into ring. Join with sl st to top of first dc. **Rnd 2** Ch 2 (does not count as 1 dc), [1 dc in next dc, 2 dc in next dc] 9 times, 1 dc in last dc—28 dc. Join with sl st to top of first dc. **Rnd 3** Ch 2, 1 dc in each of first 2 dc, [2 dc in next dc, 1 dc in next dc] 13 times—41 dc. Join with sl st. **Rnd 4** Ch 2, 1 dc in first dc, [2 dc in next dc, 1 dc in next dc] 20 times—61 dc. Join. **Rnd 5** Ch 2, 1 dc in first dc, 2 dc in next dc, 1 dc in next dc, [2 dc in next dc, 1 dc in each of next 4 dc] 11 times, 2 dc in next dc, 1 dc in each of last 2 dc—74 dc. Join. **Rnd 6** Ch 2, 1 dc in each of first 4 dc, [2 dc in next dc, 1 dc in each of next 4 dc] 14 times—88 dc. Join. **Rnd 7** Working in dc, inc 14 dc evenly around (having 1 more dc between incs) as before—102 dc. Join. **Rnd 8** Rep rnd 7—116 dc. **Rnd 9** Rep rnd 7—130 dc. **Rnd 10** Working in dc, inc 12 dc evenly around— 142 dc. **Rnds 11 and 12**

Work even in 142 dc. **Rnd 13** Ch 4, *skip 1 dc (or st), 1 dc in next dc (or st), ch 1; rep from * end sl st in 3rd ch of ch 4. **Rnd 14** Ch 1, sc in each dc and ch 1 sp around. Rep last 2 rnds for mesh pat 16 times more. Then rep rnd 14 (sc every rnd) for 5 more rnds. Fasten off.

FLAP

With smaller hook, ch 26. **Row 1** Sc in 2nd ch from hook and in each ch to end—25 sc. Rep row 1 until piece measures 6½"/16.5cm from beg. Dec 1 sc each end of next 5 rows. Working around outside edge of flap, work 1 sc evenly around entire outside edge, working 3 sc in each corner. Fasten off.

FINISHING

Pin pieces to measurements and steam lightly. Cut lining fabric to match bottom circle, the inside tube of bag and the flap, leaving ½"/1.25cm for seam allowances and 1"/2.5cm at top. Sew sides into tube, sew base circle into tube. Press under seam allowance at top. Tack to bag ½"/1.25cm below top. Sew lining to flap. Cut 4 lengths of yarn to make a 40"/102cm twisted cord. Make cord and thread through top of mesh sps.

Cord stay

With smaller hook, ch 22, join with sl st to first ch to form ring. **Rnd 1** Work 1 sc in each ch around, ch 1 join. Rep rnd 1 four times more. Fasten off. Fold stay at center and tack through both thicknesses at center forming a figure 8. Place on ends of cord for holding in place.

Straps

Make 2)

With smaller hook, ch 130. Sc in 2nd ch from hook and in each ch to end. Do not turn, but working into other side (beg lps) of ch, work 1 sc in each lp to end, 2 sc in last lp. Then work 1 sc in each sc all around both sides (with 2 sc in other corner). Fasten off. Centering straps 2½"/6.5cm apart at upper center back and beg at 1 mesh row below top, sew one strap securely for about 1"/2.5cm. Centering straps at 8"/20cm apart at lower center back and sewing into 2nd dc row at bottom, sew straps securely at bottom. Sew one button to center of each bottom strap beg at 3"/7.5cm down from center back, sew straight edge of flap over straps. Sew one snap to center of flap, one snap to corresponding center front of bag.

TOTE-A-TOTE

(Continued from page 76)

along opposite side (beg ch lps), work 2 sc in first lp, 1 sc in each of next 12 lps, 2 sc in last lp—32 sts. Join with sl st to first sc. **Rnd 2** Ch 1, work 2 sc in each of first 2 sts, sc in next 13 sts, 2 sc in each of next 3 sts, sc in next 13 sts, 2 sc in last st—38 sts. **Rnds 3-8** Rep rnd 2, adding 3 sts at each end of piece (6 sts total each rnd) and having 3 more sts between incs each side every rnd —74 sts. End of bottom piece. Cut piece of plastic tubing 17½"/45cm long to fit outside edge of bottom piece. **Rnd 9** Laying plastic tubing around outside, work 1 sc over tubing and through each sc around, join.

BEG MAIN BAG

Rnds 10 and 11 Work even in sc. **Rnd 12** Ch 1, [sc in each of next 4 sts, 2 sc in next st (inc), sc in each of next 3 sts, inc 1 in next sc] 8 times, sc in each of last 2 sts—90 sts. **Rnd 13** Ch 1, sc in

first st, *insert hook 1 row below next sc and work 1 sc in this sp (for 1 sc below), sc in next st; rep from *, end 1 sc below. **Rnd 14** Ch 1, *1 sc below, 1 sc in next st; rep from * to end. Rep rnds 13 and 14 for woven pat st for 8 more rnds. **Rnd 23** Ch 1, *work 3 sts in next st, work next 17 sts in pat; rep from * 4 times more—100 sts. **Rnds 24-33** Work even in pat. **Rnd 34** Ch 1, *work 19 sts, work 3 sts in next st; rep from * 4 times more—110 sts. Work even in woven pat st until bag measures 9½"/24cm from bottom piece. Work even in sc only for 5 rnds. Fasten off.

FINISHING

Block pieces lightly. Cut lining to fit shaped base, allowing ½"/1.5cm seam allowance all around. Cut lining 13"/33cm long and 32"/81cm wide for inside of bag. Sew short

sides tog to form tube. Gather one side to fit base piece. Sew sides to base.

Chain Loop

Ch 32. Sc in 2nd ch and in each ch to end. Fold loop in half and sew securely at center back.

Straps

Make 2)

Ch 100. Sc in 2nd ch from hook and in each ch to end. Do not turn, but working into other side (beg lps) of ch, work 1 sc in each lp to end, 2 sc in last lp. Then work 1 sc in each sc all around both sides (with 2 sc in other corner). Fasten off. Centering straps at 4"/10cm on front and back, sew securely to bag for 1"/2.5cm each end. Sew on button opposite loop. Turn under top section of lining 1"/2.5cm and hand-sew to inside of bag.

BLOCK PARTY

(Continued from page 84)

turn. **Row 3** Ch 3, beg in 2nd st, inserting hook from front to back, dc in each st through back lp only, turn. Rep rows 2 and 3 for twisted loops.

Squares

In mesh st (1), make 6 with A and 4 with B. In block st (2), make 4 with B and 4 with C. In shell ripple (3), make 2 with, 2 with C and 1 with D. In ridge st (4), make 4 with D. In triple tucks (5), make 2 with A and 2 with C. In twisted loops (6), make 4 with A.

FINISHING SQUARES

As each square is complete, using same color, work 21 sc along top edge to last st, work 3 sc in next st; work in same way for other three sides, sl st to first st. With RS facing, leaving a 15"/38cm tail, join E with sc to lower left center corner st, ch 1, sc in same st, *ch 1, skip next st; rep from * along edge to corner, working sc, ch 1, sc into center corner st. Cont as established along each side, end with a ch 1 and sl st into first sc. Fasten off, leaving a 15"/38cm tail.

Joining squares

Hint Squares are connected with a rickrack st worked through the ch-1 spaces. To line up the spaces, run a small knitting needle in and out through the openings. Lay out the blocks foll the placement diagram. Work across each horizontal row, connecting the sides of adjoining squares using the rickrack edging as foll: With WS of squares tog, leaving a 15"/38cm tail, join at corner ch-1 sp with sc, sc into same sp, skip next st, *ch 1, (sl st, sc, sl st) into next ch-1 sp, skip next st; rep from * along edge to corner, ending ch 1, sl st, sc in corner ch-1 sp. With E, join the horizontal rows tog as before and also working through the ch-1 spaces of each join. Work around outside edges as before.

Chained knots

If necessary, add 15"/38cm length of E in order to have four 15"/38cm strands on the RS at each junction. With two of the four strands crochet a ch, fasten off, leaving a 3"/7.5cm tail. Rep for other 2 strands. Coil chains in a circle, fasten down with 3"/7.5cm tails. Rep for all junctions.

A1	B2	A1	B2	A1
C2	A6	C3	A6	C2
B1	D4	A5	D4	B1
A3	C5	D3	C5	A3
B1	D4	A5	D4	B1
C2	A6	C3	A6	C2
A1	B2	A1	B2	A1

DIAMOND JUBILEE

(Continued from page 88)

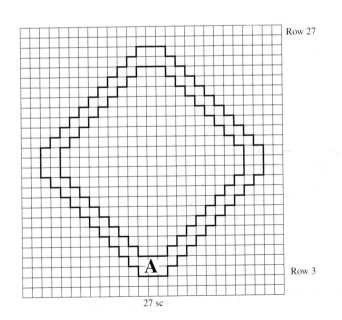

Row 27

A

Row 3

27 sc

Color Key

B = Lt. Periwinkle

C = Peacock Green

D = Emerald Green

E = True Blue

F = Paddy Green

G = Parakeet

H = Skipper Blue

D / C	H / G	F / H	D / G	C / D
F / B	G / H	B / C	C / F	G / B
B / F	D / E	E / B	G / D	E / C
F / D	H / C	F / G	C / E	H / F
C / G	B / D	E / H	D / B	G / E
B / H	G / C	D / F	B / E	E / G
H / D	F / E	B / G	F / C	D / H
C / H	H / B	G / F	E / D	C / B

GRAPHIC ART

(Continued from page 96)

with a sl st in ch-1, changing to B. **Rnds 4 and 5** Rep rnd 1. After rnd 5 is completed, fasten off.

PILLOWS

Notes

1 When changing color, draw new color through 2 lps on hook to complete sc.
2 Do not carry colors across. Use a separate skein of yarn for each color section.

CROSS PILLOW

(make 2 pieces)
With A, ch 65.
Row 1 (RS) Sc in 2nd ch from hook and in next 22 ch, with B sc in next 18 sts, with A sc in last 23 sts—64 sts. Ch 1, turn. **Rows 2-24** Sc in each st across, matching colors. Ch 1, turn. **Rows 25-42** With B only, sc in each st across. Ch 1, turn. When row 42 is completed, join A, ch 1, turn. **Rows 43-64** Rep row 2. When row 64 is completed, fasten off.

FINISHING

Place squares tog with WS facing. Sew 3 sides; turn RS out. Slip in pillow form; whipstitch opening closed.

TWO-COLOR SQUARE PILLOW

Note

To join rnd and change color, insert hook into ch-1, then draw new color through all lps on hook.

SQUARE

(make 2 pieces)
With A, ch 4. Join ch with a sl st forming a ring. **Rnd 1** Ch 3 (counts as 1 sc and ch 2), *sc over ring, ch 2 (corner sp); rep from * around 3 times. Join rnd with a sl st in 1st ch of ch-3. **Rnd 2** Ch 1 (always counts as 1 sc), *work [sc, ch 2, sc] in next corner ch-2 sp, sc in next sc; rep from * around 3 times, end [sc, ch 2, sc] in next corner ch-2 sp. Join rnd with a sl st in ch-1. **Rnd 3** Ch 1, *work [sc, ch 2, sc] in next corner ch-2 sp, sc in next 3 sc; rep from * around 3 times, end [sc, ch 2, sc] in next corner ch-2 sp, sc in next 2 sc. Join rnd with a sl st in ch-1. **Rnd 4** Ch 1, *work [sc, ch 2, sc] in next corner ch-2 sp, sc in next 5 sc; rep from * around 3 times, end [sc, ch 2, sc] in next corner ch-2 sp, sc in next 4 sc. Join rnd with a sl st in ch-1. **Rnd 5** Ch 1, *work [sc, ch 2, sc] in next corner ch-2 sp, sc in next 7 sc; rep from * around 3 times, end [sc, ch 2, sc] in next corner ch-2 sp, sc in next 6 sc. Join rnd with a sl st in ch-1. **Rnds 6-16** Cont to work 2 more sc between each cor-

ner every rnd. On rnd 16, there are 29 sc between corners and change to B at end of this rnd. **Rnds 17-32** Cont to work 2 more sc between each corner every rnd. When rnd 32 is completed, fasten off.

FINISHING

Place squares tog with WS facing. Sew 3 sides; turn RS out. Slip in pillow form; whipstitch opening closed.

THREE-COLOR SQUARE PILLOW

Note

To join rnd and change color, insert hook into ch-1, then draw new color through all lps on hook.

SQUARE

(make 2 pieces)
Work as for two-color square, but work rnds 1-9 with A, rnds 10-23 with B and rnds 24-32 with C.

FINISHING

Place squares tog with WS facing. Sew 3 sides; turn RS out. Slip in pillow form; whipstitch opening closed.

STAR STRUCK

(Continued from page 86)

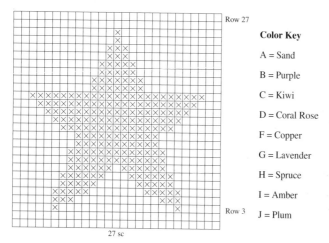

Row 27

Row 3

27 sc

Color Key

A = Sand

B = Purple

C = Kiwi

D = Coral Rose

F = Copper

G = Lavender

H = Spruce

I = Amber

J = Plum

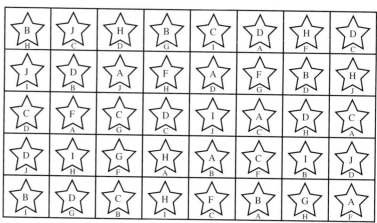

HEART WARMING

(Continued from page 98)

next 3 vertical threads of 3 rows below, work double raised dc under next vertical thread. Draw up a lp in last 2 vertical threads.

Row 7 (second half) Rep second half of row 5.
Row 8 (first half) Insert hook under 2nd vertical thread from side edge of the previous row. Yo and draw up a lp. Retaining all lps on hook, draw up a lp in each vertical thread to end.
Row 8 (second half) Rep second half of row 5.
Row 9 Rep first and second half of row 7. **Row 10** Rep first and second half of row 8. **Row 11 (first half)** Work as for first half of row 7. **Row 11 (second half)** Yo, draw through 1 lp, [yo and draw through next 2 lps on hook] 10 times, *ch 4 (bobble), [yo and draw through next 2 lps on hook] twice; rep from * 7 times, ch 4, [yo and draw through next 2 lps on hook] 12 times. **Row 12 (first half)** Work as for first half of row 8. **Row 12 (second half)** Yo, draw through 1 lp, [yo and draw through next 2 lps on hook] 11 times, *ch 4 (bobble), [yo and draw through next 2 lps on hook] twice; rep from * 7 times, ch 4, [yo and draw through next 2 lps on hook] 11 times. Cont to foll chart (working bobbles on second half of row and pushing them to RS on foll row) until row 38 is completed. Fasten off.

FINISHING

With WS facing and crochet hook, sc 2 squares tog forming a vertical strip. Rep for rem 2 squares. Sc strips tog forming pillow front. Sc front and back tog, leaving bottom edge open. Slip in pieces of batting. Stuff pillow between batting with fiberfill; sc opening closed.

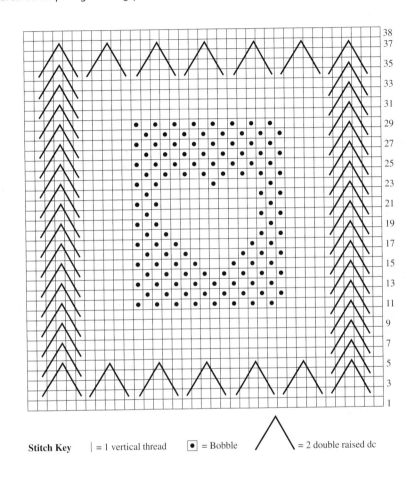

Stitch Key | = 1 vertical thread   ▣ = Bobble   ⋀ = 2 double raised dc

---

TRUE BLUE

(Continued from page 102)

ch 2, (sc, ch 2, sc) in sc; rep from *, end last rep ch 2, sc in beg ch. Ch 3, turn.
Row 3 Dc in first sc, *skip ch-2 sp and sc, sc in ch-2 sp, skip sc and ch-2 sp, shell in next ch-2 sp; rep from *, end last rep skip sc and ch-2 sp, 2 dc in beg sc. Ch 1, turn.
Row 4 Sc in first dc, *ch 2, (sc, ch 2, sc) in next sc, ch 2, (sc-ch 2, sc) in ch-2 sp; rep from *, end last rep ch 2, sc to top of beg ch. Ch 1, turn.
Row 5 Sc in first sc, *skip ch-2 sp and sc, work shell in next ch-2 sp, skip sc and ch-2 sp, sc in next ch-2 sp; rep from *, end last rep skip sc

and ch-2 sp, sc in beg sc. Ch 1, turn. **Row 6** Rep row 2. Ch 1, turn.

Row 7 Sc in first sc, *ch 2, (sc, ch 2, sc) in ch-2 sp of (sc, ch-2, sc) of previous row; rep from *, end ch 2, sc in beg sc. Fasten off. In same way, work border along opposite side. With RS facing, join A to corner of lengthwise border and work 11 sc across border, 123 sc along width of piece, 11 sc along rem border 145 sc. Work rows 1-7 of border as before. In same way, work border along rem side. Fasten off.

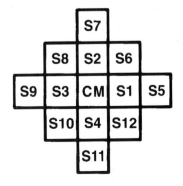

THE GREAT INDOORS

(Continued from page 100)

end work 3 dc in same ch-2 sp, ch 2. Join rnd with a sl st in 3rd ch of ch-3. Fasten off. **Rnd 3** With A, rep rnd 2. **Rnd 4** Join B with a sl st in any corner ch-2 sp, ch 3, work 2 dc in same sp, ch 4, sl in 3rd ch from hook (picot made), ch 1, ** +work 3 dc in next ch-1 sp, ch 4, sl in 3rd ch from hook, ch 1; rep from + to next corner ch-2 sp, work (3 dc, ch 4, sl st in 3rd ch from hook, ch 1, 3 dc) in same sp; rep from ** around to beg half corner, end work 3 dc in same ch-2 sp, ch 4, sl in 3rd ch from hook, ch 1. Join rnd with a sl st in 3rd ch of ch-3. Fasten off.

PLACEMENT DIAGRAM

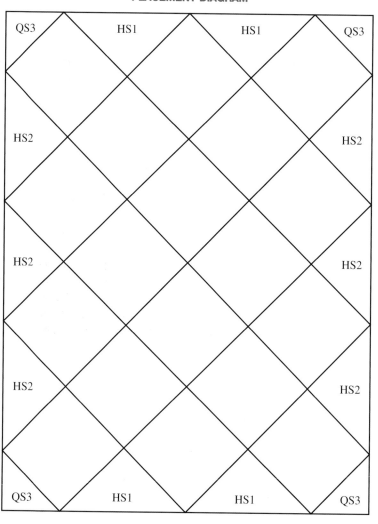

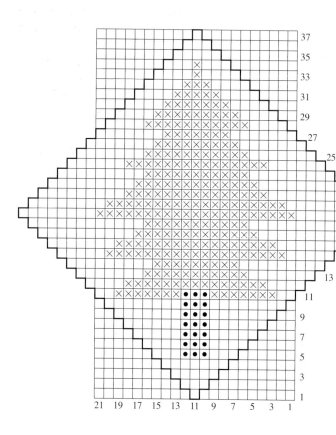

Color Key

☐ Fisherman (MC)

⬤ Brown (A)

☒ Pine (B)

HAT TRICK

(Continued from page 108)

both lps of each st around, join to any center dc of dc-double-inc. Ch 1, sc in same st, *sc in each of next 3 sts, work sc-double-dec as before, sc in each of next 3 sts, work 3 sc in next st for sc-double-inc; rep from * around end with only 2 sc in same st as first, join with sl st to beg sc, fasten and end off.

Rnd 4 With WS facing and C, working through both lps of each st, join to any center sc of sc-double-inc. Ch 1, sc in same st, *sc in each of next 3 sts, work sc-double-dec as before, sc in each of next 3 sts, work 3 sc in next st for sc-double-inc; rep from * around end with only 2 sc in same st as first, join with sl st to beg sc, fasten and end off. **Rnd 5** With RS facing and D, rep row 4. **Rnd 6** With WS facing and A, working through both lps of each st, join to any center sc of sc-double-inc. Ch 1, sc in same st, *hdc in each of next 2 sts, dc in next st, +yo hook and pick up lp in next st, yo hook and draw through 2 lps+, skip next st, rep from + to +, yo hook and draw through all 3 lps on hook for dc-double-dec, dc in next st, hdc in each of next 2 sts, sc in next st; rep from * around end without last sc, join with sl st to beg sc—64 sts.

Row 7 (RS) Ch 1 and turn, *hdc in each of next 2 hdc, work dc-double-dec as before, hdc in each of next 2 hdc, sc in next sc; rep from * around, join with sl st to beg hdc, fasten and end off—48 sts.

Small checkerboard pat

With RS facing and B, join to any st. Ch 3 (counts as a dc). Working through both lps of each st, dc in each of next 3 sc, changing to D at last st, *with D, dc in each of next 4 sc, changing to B at last st, with B, dc in each of next 4 sc, changing to D at last st; rep from *

around, end with 4 dc in D, changing to B at last st, join with sl st to top of beg ch-3.

Next row (RS) With B, ch 3 (counts as a dc). Working through both lps of each st, dec next 2 dc tog, dc in next dc, changing to D at last st, *with D, dc in next dc, dec next 2 dc tog, dc in next dc, changing to B at last st, with B, dc in next dc, dec next 2 dc tog, dc in next dc, changing to D at last st; rep from * around, end with dc in next dc, dec next 2 dc tog, dc in next dc in D and changing to B at last st, join with sl st to top of beg ch-3—36 sts. **Next row (WS)** With B, ch 3 (counts as a dc). Working through both lps of each st, dc in each of next 2 dc, changing to D at last st, *with D, dc in each of next 3 sc, changing to B at last st, with B, dc in each of next 3 sc, changing to D at last st; rep from * around, end with 3 dc in D, join with sl st to top of beg ch-3, fasten and end off both yarns.

Welt

With RS facing and C, join to any st, ch 1 and sc in each dc around, join with sl st to first st.

Next rnd (WS) Ch 1 and turn, sc in each st around, join to beg, fasten and end off.

Cone

With RS facing and E, join to back lp of any st, ch 1.

Rnd 1 (RS) Working into the back lp of each st, sc in each st around—36 sc. From here on do NOT join rnds, but work circularly marking beg/end of rnd with contrasting colored yarn, RS faces always. From here on, always work through both lps of all sts.

Rnd 2 *Sc in each of next 4 sc, dec next 2 sts tog; rep from * around—30 sts. **Rnd 3** and all odd rows Sc in each st around. **Rnd 4** *Dec first

2 sts tog, sc in each of next 3 sc; rep from * around—24 sts. **Rnd 6** *Sc in each of next 2 sc, dec next 2 sts tog; rep from * around—18 sts. **Rnd 8** *Dec first 2 sts tog, sc in next sc; rep from * around—12 sts. **Rnd 10** *Dec next 2 sts tog; rep from * around—6 sts. **Rnd 12** Sc in every other st around—3 sts. **Rnd 13** Skip first st, sl st in next st, fasten and end off.

TOP TASSEL

With F, wrap around 4"/10cm piece of cardboard several times, tie at top end tightly leaving 4"/10cm tails, cut other end. Unravel ends to tassel to fray. Attach to top of hat.

BOTTOM TRIM

With F, wrap around 4"/10cm piece of cardboard several times. With any Wool-Ease color and smaller hook, ch into each consecutive wrapped lp to one edge of cardboard to "catch" and fasten strands. As these are worked, you may slide them off and remove them from cardboard to free up space for more lps. Work until chain loosely fits around bottom ribbing of hat. Join with sl st to first ch, fasten and end off Wool-Ease. If desired, run these lps through sewing machine catching lps just below crocheted ch.

Cut open-looped end of F (the unchained end). Fray as before. Sew ch to bottom of hat with ch hidden to inside just above bottom edge of ribbing, easing in fullness.

TIES

With F, make two twisted cords 18"/45.5cm long. Make two tassels as before, attach to one end of each cord. Tack each tie to opposite ends of hat at bottom edge.

EASY ACCENTS

(Continued from page 112)

Rnd 17 With B, work even on 27 clusters.
Rnd 18 With C, work even on 27 clusters.
Rnd 19 With E, ch 1, *1 sc in each of 2 dc, 1 sc in ch-1 sp, 1 sc in each of 2 dc, 1 sc in ch-1 sp;

rep from * around. Join with sl st to first sc.
Rnd 20 With E, ch 1, *work 1 sc in each of next 3 sc, ch 3, sl st in first ch (for picot); rep from * around. Fasten off.

SWEET DREAMS

(Continued from page 110)

PLACEMENT DIAGRAM

C, B, A	A, C, B	D, A, C	B, MC, A	D, MC, B	C, B, A	B, MC, B	A, D, A
A, C, B	C, A, D	B, MC, A	C, A, B	A, D, A	MC, D, C	A, D, A	MC, C, B
B, MC, A	MC, D, B	C, A, D	B, MC, A	C, B, D	D, A, B	B, MC, D	C, B, A
C, A, D	D, A, C	A, C, B	MC, D, C	D, MC, B	B, C, A	MC, C, B	B, A, C
D, A, B	B, MC, A	C, A, D	D, A, B	A, C, A	MC, D, B	C, D, A	D, B, D
MC, D, C	A, B, D	MC, D, B	A, B, A	MC, C, B	C, B, A	MC, D, C	B, MC, A
B, C, A	D, MC, B	B, C, A	C, B, D	D, A, C	MC, D, B	C, B, A	A, C, D

Color Key

Lt pink (MC)

Mint (A)

Mango (B)

Yellow (C)

Apricot (D)

PRETTY IN PINK

(Continued from page 116)

between [ ]'s once, end ch 1, skip 3 dc, in next sp work (3 dc, ch 1, 1 dc, 1 hdc, 1 sc), sl st to next dc. Fasten off.

3/4 SQUARE (right seam edge)

Work basic square rnds 1-3.

Row 4 In first corner, work (1 sc, 1 hdc, 1 dc, ch 1, 3 dc); [ch 1, skip 3 dc, 3 dc in next sp] twice, ch 1, skip 3 dc, in next sp work corner, rep between [ ]'s twice, ch 1, skip 3 dc, in next sp work corner, ch 1, skip 3 dc, 3 dc in next sp, ch 1, skip 3 dc, 3 dc in next sp, sc in next sp. Fasten off.

SLEEVES

Row 1 squares

Joining squares as before; join ½ square, 2 basic squares and ½ square. **Row 2 of squares** Work as for row 1 of squares. **Row 3 of squares** Joining squares as before, join ¾ square right seam edge, 2 basic squares and ¾ square left seam edge. **Rows 4 and 5 of squares** Join 4 basic squares across (a total of 14 basic squares in each sleeve).

Side seam edge

Working along joined squares of sleeve and one side seam edge, work as foll: **Row 1** Join at top of row 5 of squares and work 1 dc in side of each st on square of row 5, 1 dc in side of each st on square of row 4, 1 hdc in side of each st on square of row 3 and sc in square of row 2, eliminate row 1, ch 1 and turn. **Row 2** Work sc in row 2, hdc in row 3, dc in rows 4 and 5 as before. Fasten off. Work edging along other seam edge in same way.

FINISHING

Block to measurements. Sew shoulder seams for 2 squares each side, leaving center 3 squares open for neck. Place markers at 6¾"/17cm down from shoulders. Sew sleeve to armholes between markers. Sew side and sleeve seams. Work an edge of sc evenly around sleeve cuff, lower and neck edges.

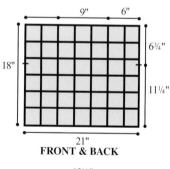

FRONT & BACK

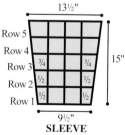

SLEEVE

Resources

We have made every effort to ensure the accuracy of the contents of this publication.
We are not responsible for any human or typographical errors.

Acknowledgements

The editors of Easy Crochet would like to thank the many people who contributed to the making of this book. First and foremost, we would like to thank the previous editors of *Family Circle Easy Knitting* magazine including Nancy J. Thomas, Carla Scott, Margery Winter and Gay Bryant. In addition, we would like to extend our gratitude to Barbara Winkler, Susan Ungaro-Keller and Diane Lamphron from *Family Circle* for their vision and support. Our appreciation also goes out to all the knowledgeable *Family Circle Easy Knitting* staff members, past and present, for their tireless efforts, skills and hard work in bringing the best of knitting to their readers. Special thanks also goes out to the dedicated knitters and contributing experts, without whom the magazine would not be possible.

Photo Credits

Paul Amato
(pp. 9, 13, 15, 19, 21, 23, 39, 47, 51, 59, 67, 109, 115)

Andy Cohen
(pp. 103)

Dan Howell
(pp. 31, 119)

Eye[4]Media
(pp. 101, 111, 121)

Brian Kraus
(pp. 75, 77, 85, 91, 93, 95)

Francis Milon
(pp. 65, 69)

Nick Norwood
(pp. 53, 57, 61, 73, 79, 81)

Novita/Finnish Press Agency
(pp. 27, 35, 41)

Marco Zambelli
(pp. 29, 37, 43, 49, 55, 71, 87, 89, 97, 107, 117)

VNU Syndications
(pp. 99, 113, 123)